THE TRAIN BEFORE DAWN

The Train Before Dawn

Janice Elizabeth Huszar

ELM HILL

A Division of
HarperCollins Christian Publishing

www.elmhillbooks.com

The Train Before Dawn

Published in Nashville, Tennessee, by Elm Hill, an imprint of Thomas Nelson. Elm Hill and Thomas Nelson are registered trademarks of HarperCollins Christian Publishing, Inc.

Elm Hill titles may be purchased in bulk for educational, business, fund-raising, or sales promotional use. For information, please e-mail SpecialMarkets@ ThomasNelson.com.

All Scripture quotations, unless otherwise indicated, are taken from the ESV˙ Bible (The Holy Bible, English Standard Version˙). Copyright © 2001 by Crossway, a publishing ministry of Good News Publishers. Used by permission. All rights reserved.

Library of Congress Cataloging-in-Publication Data

Library of Congress Control Number: 2019910458

ISBN 978-1-400327096 (Paperback)
ISBN 978-1-400327102 (eBook)

"This book is dedicated to my father, John Frank Huszar, his beloved grandsons, John Bradley Hedgepeth and Brett Latham Hedgepeth, and his great grandsons, Brennan Latham Hedgepeth, William Ashby Hedgepeth, and Lincoln Bradley Hedgepeth."

CONTENTS

PART ONE

PART TWO

PART ONE

This is my father's story. He didn't write it: he lived it, honorably and patiently through childhood, managing his little life alone on the streets of Coney Island. He became a survivor at age five, experiencing horror, betrayal and later the pain of illusive love. The love story alone is of the intense agony and absence suffered similarly by Father Ralph and Meggie, and deeper still, Heathcliff and Cathy.

His mother had just died and he missed her without relief. Even his aunts were too far away now. His father had taken him from his bed in the deep dark of night, headed for the glossy page promise of neon happiness and a sweeping beach along the Atlantic shore.

But they offered no cure for the emptiness in a room behind a shoe store. Father and son had had fun finding a place to live, enjoying a day together.

Next morning, Papa was gone.

And Mama only a memory.

She had taught Johnny to say his prayers in Hungarian, and then every night thereafter they would say their prayers together. She created an aura of love that surrounded him then, and sustained him later. The bond never faded from a little boy's memory or was ever far from a grown man's heart.

CHAPTER I

Today there is sadness and strife where once, not very long ago, there was harmony and optimism in the home, a hamlet deep in the valley of the rugged western Pennsylvania Allegany/Appalachian mountain range. It is 1918. Autumn.

The grey paint-chipped screen door squeaks open as Johnny retreats to his favorite spot, the back steps, to escape the sounds inside. He settles on the bottom one, splintered and shaky, still warm from late afternoon sun. He loves his backyard, the grapevines so good for hide and seek, the honeysuckle, the apple tree even though Mama said it is sick and don't eat any, and he wishes his house could sound happy again, like the day of his party.

She had swirled around with flowers in her hair, like a princess in a book, dancing, playing with the little children, pouring lemonade. He knew he had the best Mama in the whole world.

"Here, sweetheart, blow out your candles," she said, and in one breath he got all six. "Wow, you're so powerful. And I love you so much," he remembers her whispering into his ear. But today the children aren't here, only lots of grown-ups, and Mama is sleeping in a box by the front window.

She had been so beautiful in her lavender organdy dress that summer day. He knew about colors, but not about organdy until then. To him it looked like she wore clouds pulled down from the sky.

She was smiling. She was clapping. She had baked him a chocolate cake and made tiny cowboys and Indians to put on top. He could almost feel the delicate brush of his mother's lips as she kissed him on his cheek, wishing him happy birthday, saying again how much she loved him.

Now she can't talk with tape across her mouth.

#

There are holy people wearing long black dresses and dress-up suits in the parlor who hardly speak. Papa's friends who talk loud all the time are whispering. Others just sit on the divan or wooden chairs lining the wall shaking their heads and crying. Papa is pounding the dining room table, looking bad [sic] at Aunt Roza while raising his voice far up to say, "No, no, no!" And Aunt Agi is hollering for her salts.

Johnny wants to do something to stop the octave climb, and to try to be kind to the somber visitors in the parlor, to make them smile instead of cry. He thinks maybe he should ask if they will [sic] want some lemonade, like Mama would if she could get [sic] awake ... but then he giggles to himself: that won't work 'cause lemonade is so sour they couldn't smile anyway. Instead he will find Papa and ask him to "please talk nice to Aunt Roza." They're standing in the hallway, too close to his mother's upright piano, Johnny fears. Their faces look so scary that he shivers, afraid "they might really punch at each other and hurt the piano that Mama loves to play and is teaching me too; and what if they bang on it and break the keys, and then no more music, and maybe we can't ever play together again, and...."

"Oh, no, don't be so loud like that, Papa, please, please," Johnny begs as he moves closer to pull on his father's jacket. "And please don't cry, Aunt Roza...." But neither hears his breaking voice. It was not so much their words that frightened him: it was the shrill, the fever-pitch emotion: his Papa now huffing and puffing, and Aunt Roza making sounds like animals hurt in the woods.

The tempo quickens. Mourners begin to leave. The little boy shudders, and two church ladies fan Aunt Agi.

Johnny tiptoes over to where his mother lay, in front of the window with the fancy white lace. The room is almost empty now so he has a chance to pull the little chimney stool close to her; he climbs up, stands alone for a minute to think, and wonders ... "Will the doctors that made Mama better before come back? "Should I try to wake her up? No, not now. She would not want to hear her sisters cry."

Because he can't quite reach over the side of the pine casket enough to bend down to kiss his mother goodnight, he blows a feather kind of kiss toward her. Then he steps down from the stool, but gets right back up again.

"She will like it if I say my Hungarian prayers to her."

After his last moments with his mother, though unknown to him then, Johnny moves quietly down the hall, away from his aunt and father, to the kitchen that always smells so good, and pours a cup of milk from the curvy glass bottle in the icebox. "Be careful not to drop it," Mama would always say, and he gently replaces it. He reaches for a cookie, store bought, and now in residence at the little square canister he helped paint in rainbow colors one drizzly day, and dips. The milk is cold and always the best way to enjoy a cookie. But he can tell right through the milk that it isn't his mama's cookie. They're all gone: run out. Not for long, though: as soon as she gets better, she will want to bake again.

The snack finished, Johnny heads toward his bedroom near the top of the stairs. Along the way he can hear Papa and Aunt Roza's voices, maybe a little lower now but still ugly sounding, when all of a sudden he hears his very own name. "That's me they're talking about! Over and over, higher and higher they say Johnny. Why?" With his back pressed against the hallway wall, he slides by unnoticed and hides behind the stairs where he tries to listen and understand why they are so angry.

"I try not to be bad, like those boys down the street that come here sometimes with their mother. They don't play very nice. Is that what Papa and Aunt Roza think about me, that I am bad like them? Do my own father and aunt really say that about me?" His lips quiver and tears trickle down his face because he knows in his heart he is good, that he tries to do the right thing for Mama and Papa.

#

The spinster aunts are determined, and believe entitled, to raise their sister's son, and Roza is presenting their case:

"You are not fit for this, Frank: a child needs woman's care; it's what Lizzie, God rest her soul, wants. Yes, maybe she loved you young as she was, but she knows it is a woman's place with the children. You work too many hours into the night, with no Lizzie to put the boy to bed. All day you are at the railroad yards and at night you are in back shed building ideas," she says with a smirk. "Inventor you say? Dreamer I say. It is not right the child should be so much alone! We cook for him, we wash his clothes, we teach him to be good Catholic. It is where he belongs. It is God's will."

The grieving father is desperate to keep his son, insisting to Roza it is his rightful position:

"I am husband! Lizzie would want I should raise the boy: he is my son—**my son!**" His voice is elevated with emphasis on my son, my son.

Little Johnny nods his head, half smiling, talking to himself: "How silly what Papa says…. For sure Aunt Roza knows I am his son." Tired, rubbing his eyes, he's ready now to go upstairs.

Roza continues to berate Frank for the time he spends alone with his tools: "It is hobby, not even real work, just ideas; always having big idea for invention to make world better," she says with disdain. She's trembling from emotion but isn't ready to give up.

Agi's church friends, uncomfortable near such a private matter, join the others who are departing the wake, leaving her to fan for herself. She moves quickly to her sister's side.

Frank reminds the sisters how he shared his wife, and life, with them, they having no husband or children of their own.

"I even pay for you to come to this country. First you, later you," he says as he points a finger toward each. "How do I do it? With dollars I make at my railroad job. I work hard for years, am promoted from machinist to car builder. For this we go to Philadelphia, but later we return because Lizzie wants 'to be near her sisters.' I work hard, two ways: railroad yards and in my shop. And I invent. Have patents. I can show you."

"And you see how I am generous to your no-good brother, too, when he comes for food and bed in between his magic shows—a backwoods entertainer, and where he is now? I know he always comes back for help. He's the dreamer; going to make it big on vaudeville stage," he says. "Hah!"

"And I don't like he acts the big shot with all that trickery in front of my son! He gives him ideas. No more. I protect him. I am a good man: took care of the wife and her family, and I will take care of my son."

The sisters are not listening.

#

In a child's world, visits from a showman uncle with embellished stories of travel and magic tricks would be enchanting, seductive. It's not surprising my father remembered the man who promised to teach him the harmonica, and take him along on the circuit one day as part of his act.

Roza announces that she's now head seamstress at Sol Marks Clothing making steady money.

"So you see I can take care of Johnny: God knows I love him like my own. We both do—tell him Agi," she says with a nudge.

Looking directly into Frank's sad eyes, Agi takes a deep breath and with defiance in hers, says: "Yes, we do. Like our own we do. Lizzie knows it too. Her boy belongs to us now."

#

The sisters are simply unrelenting, further provoking conversation so out of place in the home of a grieving man that Frank can take no more. He orders them to leave.

"Get out of my house, both of you! My son stays with me. We manage alone."

They stand stunned for a moment, and because they are in mourning and wear only long-sleeved black dresses, Frank silently offers each a heavy wool sweater and scarf to protect against the evening chill. They grab the garments without acknowledgment and stalk out.

Together they walk the dark dirt road to the house they share at its end. And even after Frank's dismissal, the sisters remain deliberate and have no fear of defeat. They intend to enlist the townspeople, their friends who love Johnny, and of course, Father Hudek, to pressure this selfish man Lizzie should have had the sense not to marry. Yes, their priest will make it right.

Frank isn't faithful to the church: only goes to Mass on high holy days and what kind of an example is that for a young boy? A man alone, sinner in the eyes of God, maybe liking his schnapps a little too much … oh no! No! That is no place for Johnny. Everyone knows that.

They go to sleep with a thankful heart, confident they will soon have him as their own.

CHAPTER II

It was soon after his mother had been moved from the window resting place to a new home where "she can be happy and not ever sick and have angels for friends, and will wait for me there," Papa says, that Johnny felt the heavy breath of his father on his face stirring him from sleep.

Frank whispers in his ear, "Johnny Boy, wake up, open eyes." He shakes his sleepy son: "Come on, come on, big boy, get up; you will like: we go on train." He grabs some clothing and tries to dress the child.

"Hurry, we must go before light."

"Where are we going, Papa?"

"I just told you: to the train."

"Here, put these on. No, no, over your nightclothes. And these shoes…. Now hurry. The train comes soon."

"Yes, Papa."

When he finishes with the last button on his cardigan, he turns and stands straight, looking up at his father, haunting hazel eyes beseeching the man to explain. But Frank quickly scoops him up in one arm, the blanket roll of personal possessions in the other, and flees from the back door, so as not to be noticed, to the railroad tracks down by the river where they will climb aboard the Pennsylvania Railroad (PRR) passenger train.

Father and son were last seen by Mr. Whitman, guardian of local lore, as he sat sentry at his kitchen window, a typical early morning routine, dawn soon to break, and watched curiously the silhouette of escape.

"Are we going to see Mama?"

"No."

"But Papa, you said she's waiting for me."

"I know what I say. But it is not now."

"Will we come back home soon, Papa? Cause I didn't say good-bye to Aunt…."

"No. We leave too early for good-bye. They sleep. We have train to catch."

The whistle sounds, and the man holding tight to his son hurries through the mountain morning mist with its daily promise of dawn, leaving forever their home, family, and beloved town with a name Johnny will one day be unable to recall.

"We sit here," Frank says, throwing the blanket roll onto the overhead shelf. He pats the weathered seats as invitation: "You put head here, feet here," he says, positioning the boy to spread out by the window and go back to sleep. He covers him with his overcoat.

"I sit over here facing you. Now close the eyes." And the little boy tries.

"I think I should sit up," Johnny says as he wiggles his way out from under the coat not many minutes later. "I don't want to miss anything. And Papa, which way will the train go?"

"Why you want to know?"

"Because one of us is backwards and I don't want it to be me."

"So why that matters, Johnny?"

"'Cause I want to see everything first, not after."

They switch.

"When can we start, Papa?" He's excited now, wide-awake, and calls out 'All aboard!' for everyone in the car to hear. The conductor turns and smiles down the aisle to the father.

"Ah ha, now we go," Frank says a minute or two later. The engine booms and the clanking begins. He wants the boy to quiet down and go back to sleep, but already his face is pressed against the window.

"Nothing out there to see yet, Johnny. Not till sun comes up and world is awake."

"But tell me where we're going, Papa."

"It is secret," my son.

"I won't tell."

"I mean it is surprise."

"I don't want a surprise. I just want to know. Please, Papa."

"I promise it is best place in the world—has circus, carousel that rides round and round, and rollercoaster that goes way up and down; a big Ferris Wheel to ride on and see everything from up high, plus all kinds of fun rides, real pony rides, mechanical metal horses to race, and…."

"What do you mean, Papa?"

"Yes, is [sic] true: mechanical horses race on metal rails. And is [sic] loud happy music all around, and fireworks and games, big blue ocean with white sand: you can build sand castle. It is [sic] place everybody saves money for all year long to take the family for fun. I see pictures in newspaper. From far away they bring children; hours and hours they drive, maybe have to stay overnight, just to spend one day."

"Oh, Papa, can we spend one day?"

"Better than that, my son; we soon live there."

"Oh boy! Really? Wow! For how long, Papa?"

"I don't know. Forever maybe. Now stop so many questions."

"I'm hungry, Papa."

"Me too, my boy. Come, we go to food car."

CHAPTER III

"Try a little mustard on it," the straggly bearded vendor suggests after handing a fresh hot dog, paper wrapped, to the young boy who wanders wearily the streets and midways of Coney Island.

Thereafter, each day when the old man is ready to close his cart, the hungry child appears and accepts without shame cold, often shriveled, hot dogs from the street corner kitchen.

The boy is scrawny for sure, and malnourished Abe figures, so he is glad to do something to keep a kid from starving. But it's the boy's gratitude, genuine—"You can't fool me; this kid is for real"—that endears Johnny to the man who becomes his first friend.

Abraham Edleman, stooped with age, watches the young boy change with age. Weeks turn into months, a year, maybe two, or could even be more, he's beginning to think; certainly much too long that Johnny's been coming around, poor kid. Somebody should do something.

"What about school, Johnny?" Abe asks kindly with concern. "You gotta [sic] start, you know. It's wrong you don't go. When's your papa coming back?"

"Soon, Mr. Abe. Don't worry. He has to work, you see. He builds things, you know. He was making big railroad cars back home. Now he has to go farther to find the work."

Between infrequent unpredictable 'appearances'—so sad a definition—of his father, Johnny exists on the generosity of the man with the cart, the kindness of Mrs. Zimmerman, and his own acute instincts. He really likes Mrs. Zimmerman, the neighbor next door who has agreed to check on him occasionally, and he wishes he could stay with her always. He can understand, though: she has four children and a hardworking husband, so they couldn't take him in he heard her tell Papa. Sometimes she would bring him food she'd just cooked, and it tasted very good every time. When she made her own cookies, she would save him some.

Johnny always has peanut butter and saltines on the only shelf in the room, "just to be sure," Papa says. And then there are those famous French fries stuffed in paper cone containers that soon succumb to the heavy oil and wilt, releasing morsels of delight if one is in the right place at the right time. That would be Johnny.

Abe is intrigued by his little friend's ingenuity and amused at the choreography involved.

Johnny's strategy: "I watch the people buying fries at the stands and sometimes there are so many they fall over the edge of the paper. Or other times the bottom of the paper's so greasy from the fries it falls apart, and then the whole thing gets throwed [sic] away. That's the best, 'cause there's always some left inside. For the ones that tumble over, I just wait, but not too close, to see where they land. If it's on a cart or a bench or a ledge, something that Mama would say is clean enough, and the person walks away, then I hurry to pick'em [sic] up. But I don't want to be pushy, 'cause that would mean I'm greedy."

Abe is impressed, even proud, of the little guy.

"How did you get so smart so young?" he asks with a smile behind the signature salt and pepper beard.

"I don't know. I just am, I guess. I think I get it from my papa."

"Well, he must be very proud of you."

"I guess … I think he is, because he works so hard for me."

"I see," Abe says gently but hesitantly, wanting really to admonish the boy for the sins of his father. He would like to have said, "Tell your papa to get a job around here, even if it's not the same work he wants. It's more important he be with you than way out wherever he is."

But these are words he cannot say to the boy.

"I think so too," Abe softly agrees. "And what I see with this little French fry dance you do is that you use observation and precision, and know not to be intrusive."

"Yes, sir. I think you're smart too, Mr. Abe. But … well, just what is intrusive? What does it mean?" Reluctant to ask too much at once, he decides to delay the precision query.

"Okay, let's see… In this case intrusive means not being pushy or greedy, just like you said. Not getting too up-close to somebody, not forcing yourself on anyone, like going into a party when you're not invited. You, young man, are being polite," Abe says. "You are well mannered."

"Thanks, Mr. Abe," says the little boy more starved for praise and attention than food. Quite self-sufficient, he manages to satisfy the tummy, but never the hunger.

Only Papa can fix that.

Unlike the first sanctuary behind the shoe store, Johnny's new home is the garret of a Victorian structure, conspicuous in orange and bright blue, with borders of beet red, that serves as a lodging house. A boarding house would include meals; this does not.

Just far enough away from Coney Island's neon lights and the noise of Surf Avenue to claim residential property, the new residence allows the summer sounds to arrive on a softer pitch.

Most likely the father had wanted something more familiar, a neighborhood, for Johnny. The move occurred early, suggesting perhaps Frank knew his absences would increase. The tight quarters were punishing and the parade of short-term occupants disturbing, but still it was better than being surrounded by shoes.

Johnny doesn't know anyone except the people next door: that nice lady, Mrs. Zimmerman, who always smiles and the man who does not. He probably has to hurry to a job he hates: and they are very busy people with babies and older children who always go to school but never come out to play. Johnny can't wait to go to school and hopes the next time his father comes home will be his time to start. He already knows the alphabet and numbers, and is well into teaching himself to read: his phonics a blend of letters and the simplicity of sounds. He likes to include new words with the familiar, always building on his vocabulary. He uses big letter headlines from newspapers and captions under pictures in magazines and catalogs to learn to spell and turn letters into words. The Mutt and Jeff comic strip is the real fun way to learn, and Sunday is the best day to find discarded newspapers that still have so much more to say. But it is also the loneliest day. "People are going to church in the morning and then back home to read their paper, I think. That could be why's it's empty outside."

To quicken his goal of finding playmates, Johnny visits every house along each side of the street on which he now lives. Not afraid to knock, he begins with a smile: "Hello, my name is John Huszar and I just moved here from Pennsylvania. Do you have any little boys I can play with?"

There was no harvest. Everyone was polite, but they had either infants or toddlers, or much older children. From the first house he approached, Mrs. Zimmerman's in fact, to the last, he received a similar disappointing response. Yet there is light at the end of the canvassing: while John may not have found a playmate, he did indeed find a friend.

As he nears home, Mrs. Zimmerman waves from her porch calling him to join her. He climbs the brick steps, but timidly.

"I just happened to be taking cookies out of the oven when you knocked earlier," she says. "That's why I needed to close the door so quickly. They're cool now. Nice soft round cake kind, half white and half chocolate on top. Would you like one, John?"

"Oh, yes, ma'am. Thank you. And you can call me Johnny."

Chapter IV

Summer nights at Coney Island are magical with iridescent skies, crystal stars dancing, band music in the streets, a city-size wonderland of amusements, and thousands of happy people all around. Mr. Abe stays open late and that makes Johnny feel safe to know his friend is near. Otherwise he is extra careful not to venture very far from home, and especially to never ever go near the Bowery and its honky-tonk. But it isn't his real home, and regardless that it stands with pride as a legitimate landscaped residence, it is still in the shadow of all that glitters.

Although Johnny is more an observer than participant, he sometimes gets swept up in summer's allure. Everything seems electrified: bigger, better, louder. There are even a few things that are free to sample in the land of fantasy, and he happily moves among the crowds without notice. Just turning six years old now—real time—his height would have been well below the adults, easy to miss or assumed to be part of a family nearby. Yet there were also many times, many crossings, where he visibly walked alone, and no one ever questioned.

It was enough to simply stand by and watch the spectacle of the many famous attractions with people swinging high in the air, riding high in the air, and metal horses on high metal racing tracks competing in and out and around a huge building. Even just inhaling seasoned air from food-stand grills is kind of fun for an easy-to-please child; sometimes he buys a sarsaparilla from the coins his father leaves behind. But Johnny always heads back home when the fireworks start. He stops on the way to say goodnight to Mr. Abe, helps him pack up, maybe enjoys a hot dog if remaining, and then under the man's watchful eye, walks the rest of the way home. That is his clock, his bedtime story, his kiss.

#

Coney Island is never completely closed during winter season, but the magic is gone for the Everyman. Not for the wealthy, however. Luxury hotels and swanky restaurants lure the upscale Manhattan elites year-round: ballrooms, theaters, fancy bathhouses, and elegant nightclubs serve their Gotham patrons through the night, all through the year. They are not a part of the believed to be plebeian storybook playground just blocks away.

Family trips to fantasy almost vanish out of season: Memorial Day to Labor Day, but they stay open on weekends when weather allows. Steeplechase and Luna Park lose their luster, leaving outside businesses to fill the void. Exotic ethnic foods beckon, tin piano tunes entertain, sultry singers add occasional talent, and revelers, ever celebrating, keep the bars and grills alive. But with most rides, games, and concession booths at rest there is little traffic along the midway and beyond: the carnival sprawl, avenues and 'walks'—as short side streets are called—seem deserted save for the few determined independent vendors.

Even the Bowery is subdued.

When days are cold and gloomy, Johnny hates to be inside alone. With Mr. Abe packing up in the afternoon now, he wishes he could go home with him. He would never ask, of course, but he wishes it.

Instead, he returns to an empty garret with its two cots and a bathroom one level down, shared by an ever-changing roster of transient tenants, and accepts his circumstances. He tries to keep his home clean. Mama always did. And it just might make Papa want to come back sooner.

There is a bathtub on funny-looking feetlike claws that Johnny scrubs for himself before a bath. Sometimes, too, he will wipe the toilet seat with wet paper if the lodgers look dirty. He likes to take a bath, especially in winter because it keeps him warm. He can pretend to swim or just play in the water. He has four little cork boats that the pretty lady with the sailorman who won lots of prizes gave him. The man liked to play the games, not for the teddy bears and baby dolls Johnny suspected, but for the big hugs he got when he hit the target and the bell rang and the pretty lady jumped up and down, and he would pick her up and swirl her all around.

Even heavy-hanging bathroom stench can't spoil the pleasure of a playful bath.

#

Regardless of repeated waiting and its consequent loneliness, Johnny never doubts his father or the importance of the trips that call him away, believing faithfully in, "Maybe just one more time and then is over." Always forgiving each broken promise, he still waits and dreams:

"Papa will be home every day, maybe making more inventions, or finding train cars to fix, and I will go to school every day, and then I will sit on his lap every night and read with him, and be so happy."

> The Lord is near to the brokenhearted
> And saves the crushed in spirit.
> Psalm 34:18

According to the notes I took from my father, his father had applied for a patent on at least two inventions, but then could never pay for them, foreshadowing his son's patent, also lost, not to inability to pay however, but to infringement.

Johnny continues to feel the need to know more about the inventions. "How do you even start to think them up? I have to find out how to begin. 'Cause I want to do that someday. But I don't know what I will want to make yet. It has to be something that is good for everybody.

"Next time Papa comes home I will surely ask him. And he will tell me everything."

#

When his father finally takes a break from his curious vocation, arriving belatedly, if not annually, the surprise is better than even a birthday party. Johnny is overjoyed. Even after the long inexcusable and horribly unhealthy separation, he remembers everything about their last conversation; all he really wants to do now is return to it and talk more with Papa about his, and his grandfather's, inventions. It pleases the father—handsome with dark brown hair peppered slightly at the temple with early grey, his countenance revealing tired eyes—that his son has eager interest in his work.

He would have preferred to rest first, delay until morning, but the boy's pleasure in making him comfortable on a cot, placing a small blanket around his shoulders, and patting a pillow to put between his back and the wall gives him renewed energy. He cannot ask the child to wait another day. Snuggled together side by side on a narrow cot, precocious little Johnny enjoys a lesson in mechanical engineering.

At that very young age he begins to understand, and embrace, the intricacies of his grandfather's creations. And being so proud of him, and his Papa, he listens and learns, and never forgets.

Many years later my father sat with me one evening and recalled golden moments with his father, explaining the mechanics of his two inventions in detail, even sketching the process of each as I hurried with a diminishing soft pencil to capture his words. It may well have been the first time my father truly realized his lineage: the inherited gift of creative invention.

#

Bright and early next morning father and son visit Morris, the grocer and sometimes banker, in his primitive straw and mud-floor market just around the corner. Frank settles up his account for the few sundries Johnny had needed, and then instead of starting another tab, this time he pays ahead.

They purchase a little milk and corn flakes and a measurement of sugar, and return to the room, Johnny still excited from last night. There is no kitchen, only bowl and pitcher serving as a sink, a tiny corner shelf, and a very small wooden end table someone had covered with a piece of blue-checkered oilcloth. It is insufficient as a dining table at only two feet high, a width not quite two feet, and barely 16 inches in depth. But Johnny sees it as perfect.

He pulls the quasi table over in between their cots, wipes the dust off the little blue-and-white boxes, and empties cereal into bowls left from former occupants and pours the milk, apportioned equally, after carefully saving some in a stubby jelly jar for drinking a little later before it turns. Each washes his hands in the lavatory below with its stand-alone sink, providing also their drinking water and use of the bathtub to all occupants of that floor and above.

Sitting as straight as possible in his most grown-up demeanor, Johnny engages his father once again on the subject of inventions.

"I really liked it when you told me about the automatic record selection, Papa," he says. "I guess 'cause I like music. And for sure if I had sixty records and a Victrola to play them, I would want to keep my records shiny and not get any scratches. So I would buy it. Lots of people would want to do that. But I like the Mechanical Impact Hand Punch too: it looks like fun.

"I bet those leather washers, or rubber washers, or sheet metal washers, or other kinds of things just pop out, pow-pow-pow, like bullets or little cannons. Wow! It must be very hard to make these kinds of things. Only very smart people can do it, I think. Hooray for your papa, and you, Papa," Johnny says, finding the repetition funny. "How do you think he learned all that?"

"It was just his way. And it is my way, too: Always I am thinking. And working with my hands. I like to find ways to make life easier and safer for people. You will understand. You are like me.

"But right now, my son, you tell me how you know about bullets!"

"Cowboys, Papa, they always have guns and bullets 'cause the Indians have arrows. They're in the picture books. I never heard them: I just know they sound loud."

"And how, I ask, that you, my son, can know...."

Johnny sees in his father's eyes the further question and quickly answers:

"I learned about cannons in a big history book that Mr. Abe gave me. He said I could know lots of things just by looking at pictures of famous people and important battles in the wars, and even in your old country too, the one with two names."

Frank smiles, "Yes, for many years it is two names but one country, Austria-Hungary. It is one of world's great powers and fought in World War till end in 1918, not very long ago. That is when we become two countries: Austrian Republic and Hungarian Kingdom.

"Your mama and me, we are both born in Austria and live in Vienna; but we are near area where many people always speak Hungarian. It is good we both grow up to speak the Hungarian. When we are children we never know each other."

"Mama taught me prayers in Hungrean [sic], Papa. I like the Hungrean [sic] way. But don't you think to call a country 'Hungre' sounds silly? It's like they have no food."

"Of course there is food, Johnny. The country is not hungry: it is Hun ga re. Do you hear the difference?"

"Yes, Papa. I do. But now I'm thinking about the war. Do you know the names of any heroes in the big World War?"

"You learn good, my son. In newspaper I see some heroes' names: There is Navy officer Edouard Izac whose ship is torpedoed and he is captured by enemy Germans but escapes from prison camp and helps others get out too; then hides in the woods heading for river. He swims River Rhine to Switzerland where he is safe. Not long ago I hear on radio he is given Medal of Honor for the bravery. Marine Sergeant Dan Daly already had two Medals of Honor from earlier war, Boxer Rebellion, and they want to give him third Medal of Honor for so much courage in World War; but it is too many they decide so honor him with Distinguished Service Cross and French Medaille Militaire. He is big hero. I do not know about others."

"Well, what do you think about Napoleon, Papa? He was one of the best warriors to lead ever, I think; my book says that. Right?"

"Is true," Frank says, nodding his head, amazed at the depth of the questions. "But the little Emperor of France was too greedy for power: marching his armies into countries of Europe to take rule of them, to build empire. Later he starts to lose battles and is sent away for exile. Should be dungeon, but is beautiful island, Elba, instead. He stays many months, then escapes. But he surprises and comes back for more fighting, then finally gets defeated at Battle of Waterloo."

"That's a funny name too," Johnny says, smiling as he jumps up and goes to the corner book pile, excited to bring out Abe's huge world history book. He sits beside his father and turns each page one by one, explaining the pictures when he can, each time looking up into his father's eyes for approval.

"Can you find a picture of the pretty island, Papa? The Ella one."

"Yes, only name is Elba. See here how to spell. Okay?" Johnny nods a 'yes' and Papa continues:

"Napoleon died on another island. After Waterloo, he was British prisoner and they exile him to Saint Helena Island way out in the ocean off coast of Africa. That's where he died."

"But he didn't go to Heaven," Johnny was quick to add. He then turns quiet for a moment or two, just sitting there, pensive, looking off toward the only window in the room while his father turns the pages away from the consequences of war.

"That's where Mama is, Heaven, isn't she, Papa? I know she isn't coming back now. It's too long ago. But she is still waiting for me like you told me she would, but up in Heaven, right? Isn't she? I will see her then, right, Papa?"

"Yes, Johnny, she waits for you there. And you will see her one day."

"Do you miss her, Papa?"

"Yes, son, I do. All the time."

"Me too. But she comes to me sometimes: I feel her right here at my heart." He demonstrates by patting his little chest.

Frank doesn't respond: he doesn't know what to say. There's a long silence. And then he reaches for his son, pulls him close, and cradles him. Words don't fit.

#

"Papa, you are the smartest man in the world. Mr. Abe is smart too, but not the kind of smart like you. Would you like to meet him? He's very nice; he would like that. Come on, let's go," and he tugs at his father's sleeve.

"Son, I cannot go with you. I must leave now; the travel is far. First I walk to new subway that takes me to Long Island railroad terminal for electric train to Jamaica, then change to steam train on mainline that goes way out on the island, Long Island. So you see how much time it takes, how tired I will be?"

"Yes, Papa. I'm sorry it will make you tired."

"Next time," the father promises. "I will meet your friend, for sure, and I will try his hot dog. It is nice he shares with you. But do not eat only hot dogs: peanut butter is good, and sometimes a fruit from Morris. What about Mrs. Zimmerman? We had nice talk last time I'm [sic] here."

"Yes, Papa, she comes to the door sometimes. Once she brought me hot soup: chicken noodle. One time she came with potato pancake, and one time pasketti [sic]. Do you really have to leave so soon? Maybe we should go and visit her first?"

"No, I go now."

Johnny will not let his father see him cry. But he does reveal his sadness by asking if this time would be the last time he would have to go away. The answer was, "I cannot know."

"But didn't you promise that soon it would be over and you wouldn't have to work so far away, Papa?"

"Yes, and I am sorry, Son, but things change; and I think maybe it happens again that I need to stay away longer." He pulls his son close for an embrace.

"Maybe I can help you, Papa," Johnny offers, so happy being held again.

"No, my son, you cannot," he says, ruffling the boy's thick brown hair. "But I like that you want to."

Johnny knows this is not the time to bring up the burning question he harbors. He doesn't want Papa to be late and miss all those trains. He will wait for the next time. What he had hoped to find out is when he will be able to enter school. But that's okay: he has Mr. Abe's book for a teacher. And it teaches him well.

He'd been thinking maybe he could go to the church school where the nuns wear those long black dresses even when they're outside with the children. It isn't very far; he would like walking to school as his neighbors do. He might even take his big history book to share with everyone.

"I come back as soon as I can, Johnny," the father promises. "Next time, maybe then it is no more after that. Here are some coins for special sweet. And when I am back, I will have coin holder and belt for you. Don't forget. They will be yours."

"Oh boy! Thanks, Papa. I always wanted a coin changer like the workers over at Coney Island have for the rides and games, and I guess maybe the booths for food too. I can't wait! Wow!"

Johnny puts on his sweater, now looking at least a size too small, and walks beside his father part of the way to the Brighton line. Before too long it's time for him to turn back. They hug and say good-bye, Our Lady of Solace ringing in the background.

He would have anyway, when Papa asked him to understand and

be patient again, but now the fun of anticipation for his very own coin changer will make waiting easier.

His hardest time is always Sunday, albeit not much different from any other day of the week for Johnny. Without school, catechism, or church attendance, each day seems the same. Except for Sunday. Sunday feels different. Maybe in the quiet of the Lord's Day he hears the Kyrie, faint in its musical plea.

"The bells sound soft like ones back home when I would walk to church with Mama."

Maybe it's because Sunday is the day amusement parks are most crowded with families holding hands and joyfully walking the midway together, sisters and brothers squealing in delight.

Whatever its root, Johnny is saddest on Sunday.

Chapter V

At bedtime when Johnny lay alone under the single lightbulb, his eyes defiantly follow the eerie shadows along the wall. He doesn't want to see them. But there is no place to hide, no parental bed in a next room to climb into.

He will just close his eyes very tight and try to think only of good things he knows about. It becomes a journey of escape, the first in a series of self-taught endurance techniques.

He concentrates on a day long ago, struggling to recapture every detail of his favorite memory, his beloved memory, of a happier time when he was in a real house, with a real backyard, and a mother holding his hand.

It was his first birthday party so he will never forget, and everything was special. Mama escorted him outside and down the steps to the guests. She was smiling the prettiest smile. He turned six then. He knew that by six candles on the chocolate frosted double-decker cake with Wild West decorations on top.

"Hold on to this memory," the little boy hears from the depth of his consciousness. It is really all he has left, and he senses its value. It becomes routine, always at night, that he preserves the memory by rethinking it, enjoying it, feeling the love in it… And he would fall asleep comforted by the visions he recreated and the ethereal presence he welcomed.

Some nights Johnny was brave enough to blacken the room. He would position his cot under the ceiling lightbulb and steady it for a step of cautious balancing with a branch broken to size, just long enough to reach up and pull the elusive string into darkness. In a way, it was less frightening to be alone in the room with the light off, relaxing in reverie, than under a light dancing as a shadowy apparition.

It happened as he was dozing, thinking about the big juicy grapes he liked to pick from those funny twisted vines way out back of the house where he and Mama and Papa once lived. It was so much fun to play hide and seek there with the other children. Who were the other children? They seemed to always be there but distant, in the memories of his mother.

All of a sudden, in the deep of darkness, he felt fear that startled him to fully awake, his body rigid, arms glued to their side, legs paralyzed in isometric tension. His lungs filled with air that he refused to exhale as he lay motionless. He willed himself to think again of those happy times: his party, his mama, birthday candles, instead of the prickly claws upon his chest. He wore only his briefs. He had no pajamas. He had no one to hear his screams.

A snout, moist and sniffing, tickled the underside of Johnny's thigh as the forager explored, and soon he could feel the sweep of its tail atop the nerve endings of his skin, a sensation so everlasting it seemed like waiting for a long freight train to pass. Instinctively he knew not to move, not to cry, as the rodent roamed his body and bed. And when he felt the horror no longer and heard not a sound, Johnny knew not to trust the silence. He listened closely, intently, staying absolutely still save resumed breathing. Finally, when he could wait no longer, he rolled over and threw up.

Every night thereafter, before his dreamlike visits to another place, another time, Johnny would kneel at his papa's empty cot and pray, "Please God, don't let the rat come tonight."

#

It was an encounter the little boy would never forget nor share with anyone, especially his father. What would be the point? Nothing good could come of it, and it would make Papa sad, the antithesis of Johnny's perceived purpose: "Making Papa happy so he will want to come home."

The intervals between father and son are no doubt unlawful, unhealthy, and cruelly uncertain. Johnny's fears are real and increase concurrent to the calendar, each day a reminder he's alone in this stretched out emptiness. That he sustains a pattern of normalcy and moves quietly, unseen, in a world too big for him is actually heroic. He isn't a runaway kid or a troublemaker, or ditching a school bell. He's not even hiding. He's waiting. That's all.

Oh, and this: he's trying to keep up with his learning so he fits in with his grade level when he gets a chance to go to school.

#

There has been no Christmas celebration: no presents, no tree, no venison and pumpkin pie. He stayed inside, mostly so nobody would know. But then he missed the joyful music.

"Was it something I did that Papa didn't like, or maybe something I didn't do I was supposed to? Or maybe it's the bullets and cannon balls I talked about? But I thought he forgived [sic] me."

His little heart is breaking.

"I need a job. That's it! I won't be so sad if I have work to do and I will make money for when I get my coin changer."

It is pure Johnny survival mode: he has faced his problem—prolonged solitary misery—and arrived at a solution: a good one, natural next step if only he were older. In new confidence and last year's wool, he bundles up and goes out to find Mr. Abe.

And sure enough there he is, still peddling his hot dogs despite the cold. He's a man who loves his job, his corner, and his 'regulars,' mostly year- round, that surround him daily. Inclement weather never matters, because if his friends are working so is he: seeing to it that they get good grub, not the day-old stuff. It was a form of generosity, but he'd never fess up to a soft side. Except when he was with Johnny it showed.

"Hey, Mr. Abe, I'm glad you're here today. Do you think it'll snow?"

"Let's hope not," he says. "Tomorrow is Friday, and we want weekenders to come out." He pauses a moment to assemble gentle questions with words bent toward kindness. "Um…," he clears his throat, "I don't see you very much now, Johnny. So how are you, big guy? Did you lose your appetite for my hot dogs? Has your papa been home for the Christmas holiday? That's why you stay away?"

"No. Papa will come soon. I'm here because I need a job. I would like to work for you."

"Oh Johnny, no, you are too young," Abe says. "You need school; that's where you should be." Abe sees the immediate mood change, and the brave attempt to fight off tears.

"Now don't be so downtrodden; you are a kid—you need to play, you need friends your own age, and you need to study. I'm not scolding you; in fact, I am thinking it's very grown-up of you, admirable at this age."

"I study, Mr. Abe. I have your history book open lots of days. And I found a little Bible book at the top of the stairs that go into where I live; I want to learn all about God and his Son, Jesus, but this one has tiny size letters that make it very hard to read. I try to, but I don't like it that way: it takes too long. I hope it's Mama's Bible from long ago, and that Papa had it in his jacket near his heart and it fell out when we were hurrying down the stairs for him leaving on time. I think so; I will save it and see if anybody left it by mistake and comes back for it. But I hope not."

Abe is hit hard by his little friend's casual use of the word *leaving*. "As if it is permissible! It is not okay! It is not natural that a parent leaves a child. And it must stop. The boy needs stability. He needs his father," he says, only to himself.

"Okay, Johnny, I know you work hard to learn. And I know how smart you are. So maybe a few hours of helping out somewhere is not a bad idea, but not for me. I'm just a one-man operation. Let me talk to Jimmy over at the games; you know the balls and pins that fall down, the little ducks that get shot out of the water, and toys that are knocked over from the arrows? Well, they all need to be picked up. We'll see what we can do."

"Oh, thank you so much, Mr. Abe! See you later, sir."

And that afternoon a smiling little boy goes home, yes to a dreary and empty attic, but less troubled, even a little proud of his presentation. It's late in the day and Johnny is hungry, reaching for his crackers and honey when Mrs. Zimmerman knocks on the door, pushing it open herself since the bowl is not all she is carrying, and hands her nutritious and tasty lamb stew to her little neighbor. It is so much more than just the warm home-cooked meal she brings to the child: it's the deeper definition of feeling cared for, feeling safe, and having someone by his side, if only for a few minutes. As the aroma, strong and tempting, begins to fill the room, Johnny places the bowl and spoon on the little side table, gingerly moving it nearer the cots where Mrs. Zimmerman now sits, motioning him over to her. He sits down on the opposite cot.

"You have good healthy food for tonight, and I want you should [sic] eat before it gets cold. I will leave you to enjoy without me watching over. But first I want to talk to you. Look here," she says, reaching into a large paper bag; "I have three heavy jackets that my firstborn boy grew past. I want you to try them on and see what is best. Go on…."

Johnny hesitates at first, shy about accepting clothes, but then looks at his generous neighbor and smiles. She deserves that. "Which do you like? This one is your size, I think," and she hands it to him. It fits perfectly, but he doesn't like red.

"I like this one, Mrs. Zimmerman: it fits, and it has a hood. Oh, yes, I really like this."

It's grey. It matches his life.

Chapter VI

When finally the absence ends, Johnny's more thankful for his father's return than for the gift he's been waiting to receive. Still cold outside he immediately fetches his blanket for Papa, dressed insufficiently in denim and a lightweight jacket dusted with unexpected snow. After the hug, the son's welcoming words, and a requisite 'glad-to-be-back with my boy,' Johnny excuses himself. "I have to go downstairs quick, [sic] but I'll come back soon, Papa."

It was the first time Johnny ever saw the kitchen, or been in any part of the first-floor owners' quarters. Only through the glass doors in the hallway at the start of the stairs did he ever see the grand mahogany room with its big, and today burning, fireplace. He doesn't dare enter there; he follows the sweet smell of apple pie to the back of the hall and pushes against the swinging door with trepidation, for he'd already heard people talking about the landlady's harsh warden ways: stern and never smiling. Incongruously, her name is Mrs. Godly. Johnny bites back his smile.

"Yes, what can I do for you, child? You are the boy upstairs in garret, huh?"

Johnny shakes his head yes.

"I see your father is home. You tell him rent is overdue; come see me."

"Yes, ma'am, but that's not why I'm here."

"State your business then," she says gruffly. "I am busy with my pies as you can see."

"Well, I don't think my papa feels good. And I was hoping maybe I could make a cup of tea down here, where you have a stove. If I can borrow some tea leaves and mix with your water and put it on your stove, it will boil and I can take it back up to him; do you think?" He's scared to death, standing there under her piercing gaze. Maybe no one has asked anything of her before. Maybe he has made a giant mistake.

"I don't usually consort with my lodgers," she says. "They have their rooms and they have their outside lives. That is our way here. My Mr. Godley, may he rest in peace, set the rules. And my boys, they followed them faithfully all the while they were growing up here. But you," she says, "you're not a child running all around in here; you give me no trouble. And you ask for your father, not for yourself. Good trait." She pauses, then slowly renders her verdict. "Yes, you may have a cup of hot tea. Only, I will do it. Go sit over there in the corner."

"Yes, ma'am, and thank you," Johnny says. He sits down in the corner by the cupboard.

Apparently something has just happened to Mrs. Godley. "Would you like some apple pie and a glass of milk, dear?" A little boy's broad smile is her answer.

"And I will send a piece of pie up with you for your father with his tea. I want my cup and dessert plate back, though. You understand?"

"Yes, I do." Johnny accepts the pie, so warm and tasty and perfect with the cold milk. He begins to think how wrong those neighbors talking about her were: "You should never talk bad [sic] about other people Mama always said. You have to get to know them first, and then you will see their [sic] goodness."

#

"Papa, look here: I have hot tea for you," and he very gently places the cup and saucer on the little table by his cot. "A piece of apple pie is outside on the floor … on a plate, so don't worry," he says, turning around to bring it inside, so happy he has something to give. After the tea and pie the father intends to engage, and, of course, the son is ever eager to get started. But first he thinks he should return the dishes to Mrs. Godley in a timely manner so she knows he can be trusted. He washes them with cake soap in the bathroom sink down below and then proudly returns the spotless dishes he dried with his shirt. He hurries back upstairs, not just for the promised gift but the longed-for conversation.

"Johnny, bring my bag over here; is something for you," the father says in rare parental pride."

John's very excited and responds accordingly: high jumps. He sees the shiny new coin changer emerge and quickly hugs his papa, then hops over to the corner where a once pickle jar now jingles with coins.

"Look, Papa," he says, holding up his little glass bank, "look at what I have saved. It's because I work now. I have a job. I help clean the stalls and sometimes I set up bottles that get knocked down for prizes or I pick up toys and arrows in the shooting games. For this I get a nickel and a dime. Soon it will be a quarter." The father manages a big smile and reaches over to pat the boy's shoulder, almost toppling the flimsy cot. Johnny's encouraged by Papa's sign of approval and sits at his feet, safe and sound in a brand-new belt.

"And after I earn more nickels, I can trade them into two for one dime, and then…," he's doing the math, "And then I will wait till I have two dimes and one more nickel and trade them for the quarter. See this, Papa," he says, pointing proudly, "the nickel here, the dime here…," but Papa doesn't see. He has begun to slip into a kind of myopic trance, lying back now, listless on the canvas cot, his eyes open but not focused.

"Oh no, Papa, don't be sick. Please." He senses his father is not a very healthy man, but in childish denial expects to make him better as their roles reverse.

"I'm going out to find some food for you, Papa." But the pale and now quivering man manages to wave away the idea of eating. "Okay, tomorrow then," Johnny says. "I will get something to make you strong. Morris will know."

#

Days passed and Johnny's attention brought improvement. He fed his father bananas and oranges, or sometimes cheese slices and salami. Morris suggested hot bouillon but that would have been too much to ask of Mrs. Godley. Corn Flakes were a delicacy when with milk, not so much dry. Johnny wants to serve the best to his papa, to build him up to being strong again. That means adding milk to the cereal. And Johnny, of course, does. They did well, father and son. They're going to be okay.

Not too long after, Frank was able to say, "You take good care of me, my son: I am well again." He reaches down from the cot, still a little damp from the breaking fever, deep into the inside pocket of his jacket, and brings forth a billfold.

"Here, Johnny, go to Morris and get us something to eat, something good that sticks to the belly," Frank says. "And if you like, a penny candy for you."

"Oh yes, I do like candy. Thanks, Papa."

They dine on pickled pig's feet, German potato salad, applesauce, and bread Morris insisted Johnny add to the order: "For strength I tell you. A man needs his bread. A little whiskey too." Coincidently, the father just happens to have some. Thank goodness for the medicinal spirits he carries in his satchel. Balancing bowls of food on their laps, father and son sit across from each other on their cots, enjoying the fullness of their feast. When finished, Johnny jumps up and over to his papa's side. He will clear the bowls later. Right now he is eager to hear, and knows he will never forget, his ancestral history, the gift one generation gives to another.

"Tell me stories about Mama, please, Papa, please. And what it's like in your old country. Where did you find Mama, here or back in Austria? Why did you come to America anyway? They were pretty pictures of the mountains and the Daniel [sic] River you showed me in the history book. Why didn't you stay living there?" So many questions, so much time lost…. The deprivation of familial storytelling and the lack of everyday in-home conversation—that natural sway of query and reply, of being informed, of sharing—has blunted Johnny's sense of belonging. He needs to attach again, and especially he needs to know more about his mother. His father will forgive him the questions, or better said, the interview.

And that night, in the garret they call home, Frank Huszar, still a little weak and appearing too emaciated for a man of his young age, takes another swallow of whiskey, places the pint on the floor, and settles back on the narrow canvas bed made comfortable by Johnny's blanket and pillow, and remembers for his son.

"I am born in Austria, your mother too, and we both live in Dobling district of Vienna, north end of city on hillside of Vienna Woods, forest rich with—how you say, hierarchical—trees and green foliage beauty, with perfect brightness of blue from the Danube that flows through our city of Vienna. There are castles, monasteries, and Gothic cathedrals that stand all along the river, or back a little between rolling hills. It is beautiful landscape. Pictures are in periodicals seen around the world, and in storybooks. But we do not know each other. It is busy city, the capital. We are on eastern edge of Alpine chain, but still near enough to behold such beauty as Austrian Alps. My father is mechanic, and teaches mechanical engineering. Sometimes he builds for family: bicycles and carts for heavy carrying. My mother is painter, watercolors and oil. She sells her work many times: they are very good. I study mechanical engineering at university. There are no sisters or brothers. "Everywhere, all around, everything is majestic people say. They come for holiday from many countries, even America, because of Vienna's imperial beauty and scholarly works of art. It is historical city of music known around the world, presenting in major cities' opera houses. The work of master painters also happens here and their canvases are sold around the world to collectors and major museums.

"I think whole of Austria is beauty inside and out. Museums tell history in ancient artifacts and grand oil masterpieces. And our mountains: I cannot find words to describe them. But I try: When you look up to the Heavens over our mighty mountains with peaks almost touching the stars, and crystal lakes sparkling in reflection, you see best of creation. Well … Adam first and then his Eve too, and the animals and the vegetation and the flowers, yes, of course, the flowers," Papa says. "You know what I mean, Son: God made everything and everybody. Us too. And the mountains we love.

"My favorite season in Austria is winter, Johnny. It is time for sledding and skiing down the winding slopes. It is very much fun. Always there is fresh snow so beautiful they call it a winter wonderland, and make picture cards—postcards—that are famous around the world. Many people come here just to ski, but we can do it every day."

Johnny is mesmerized by the unexpected details of such beauty, images already indelible on his mind, and the easy transformation from the sea level borough of Brooklyn to the towering expanse of alpine glory.

"So why did you leave, Papa?"

"I am happy in my homeland and it is all I want. It is enough for me to stay forever in my country. I will become engineer, build like my father before me and his before him. We are men of education and skill, and we belong to our city.

"Then I see your mother."

CHAPTER VII

"It is page from Brothers Grimm Fairy Tales I think as I watch her ice skating on lake, so graceful and beautiful, rosy cheeks from the cold, dark curls falling from her hood, snowflakes painting picture I will never forget. I am up close as she glides by like ballerina on skates, and I remember exactly her face, like it is yesterday."

"So what did you do, Papa? Did you wave to her? Did you skate over to her?"

"No, I am there to meet Pavlo for lager together, but I tell him go ahead and I join soon. I watch her and wonder who she can be. I don't remember her from Volksschule. But then I think maybe she was ahead of me, a maiden in upper class." He starts to drift and Johnny does not want to lose the story.

"Well, was she…?"

"Was she what?"

"The same girl all grown up from Volkshoe [sic]?"

Frank smiles, not just at his son's pronunciation, but in remembering the beauty of those days.

"Yes, my son, turns out she is that very one. She also lives in Dobling, but I never see her till that day." He reaches for his flask and takes a few lingering sips. Johnny gently removes the almost empty canteen from him and places it back on the floor.

"So then what happened, Papa? Tell me. What happened next?"

"Pavlo goes. I stay and watch her, standing alone, not minding the cold. Then as she skates around to my side, I see she is looking at me. When she sees I see her, she lowers her eyes, but when she comes around again, she looks my way and smiles; I smile back. She spins away and I know I have just seen the prettiest girl in all of Austria! As soon as she is across the lake again, I hurry to look for Pavlo. I must find my friend!"

"Why, Papa? She has smiled at you. She wants to be your friend."

"Yes, but I want to have lager with Pavlo, and hope he has skates to loan me. I find him and we go together up to his cabin: the skates are tight but will do. I do not know where mine are, since I am not on the ice for a long time. But I am ready to skate again!"

Johnny is in awe of his storybook-handsome father who is about to win the pretty princess. "She is not there when I return," Frank says, his voice saddening again as he remembers the distress of a young man newly smitten. "I go home with skates and wait until next day. I cannot sleep thinking about her."

"Wow, Papa, you didn't even know her yet."

"Yes, but I do know."

"Know what?"

"That she is only girl for me. Next day I go and she is there. She is with sister. I skate around. We smile. I go again next day and she is there alone. She smiles more now, and I finally ask her to skate beside me. It is only right that we hold hands: I don't want her to fall. She takes away her fluffy white muff and puts on little leather glove so I can reach her hand better. I take it and guide her onto ice." Johnny beams as he imagines the scene his father has just described.

"'I am Frank,' I say. 'And I am Lizzie,' she says. That is all. Then we skate. We do not speak after that, just skate around until almost dark. It is only right I walk her home. She likes that.

"We go almost every day to the lake, looking for each other. We skate, or take walks. We go to square. We share a pastry. We sit on cement bench back by the forest. We kiss."

"Papa!" Johnny squeals in embarrassment.

"Yes. We do. And we declare our love to each other."

"Really? How did you feel Papa when she said she loved you too?"

"I cannot believe it. And I am sad because I know I am not worthy of her."

"Oh yes, you are," says the son, fully immersed in that innocent moment so long ago.

"No, I do not have money, and am still in university. Her mother is teacher of piano, her father flutist in symphony orchestra. They will not want their daughter to marry man so young and without work. No, they will not allow it."

"But you did marry her because they saw how much she loved you, right?"

"No. I steal her."

"Papa, you can't steal people! But you didn't really, 'cause she wants to be with you, right?"

"Yes, she does. I'm getting tired now, Johnny; we finish another time."

"Yes, Papa, but please just a little bit more and I will surely go to sleep knowing how you and Mama could run away from your homes, and then come all the way over to this side of the world. All that deep water and big waves to cross: even in big ships, it's too big to conquer. And I think people are supposed to stay where they are born."

Frank finds his son's pronouncement amusing, but answers seriously: "No, we are free to move to wherever we are welcome, to any country with open border and no war." He has also picked up on his son's new favorite word…. "*Conquer* you say? This is word I never hear you use before, Johnny."

"Oh yes, Papa, it's from the big history book I showed you. You saw the pages about wars far back. And we talked about new heroes, too. I think there are heroes in every war, and we should be glad. Those bad Romans conquered lots of nations and the gladiators conquered each other, sometimes even killed animals just for sport.

"Conquer is in the Bible too, when David conquered Goliath with only one stone from his sling that hit the giant's head and knocked him face down on the ground! Then David took Goliath's own sword and cut off his head! Everybody was surprised 'cause Goliath was so big and strong, but David knew what to do. And he saved the Jewish people from the killer giant. I think he's the best hero of all.

"Okay, Papa. Yes. Good-night."

Not even thinking about breakfast, Johnny begins the next day with a question far more important to him than food…. "So you came to this country, Papa, but didn't you know it would make your mama and papa cry? Didn't you even say good-bye? And didn't Mama want to kiss her mother and father bye? Well, I guess you really can't think about that if you're trying to sneak away…."

There is no answer, no acknowledgement of such direct questions. Most likely they've made Frank uncomfortable, perhaps even ashamed for allowing the power of love to decide his future. But Johnny respects his father's avoidance, and turns his attention to unraveling the tangles of a family tree.

"Maybe my grandparents did come over here to America after all," he's thinking. "But I don't know any of them. I don't think they were ever at our house. Not even at my birthday party. 'Cause I would surely see them. I would have hugged and kissed each grandmother and grandfather over and over, and read stories with them sitting side by side." It troubles Johnny, the loss of four people he should have met: so many things they could have done together. "Could we still? Or are they dead? They might be here somewhere, but I think they wanted to always stay in their own country. I do belong to them. But I don't think they know. And I don't think they would want to come all the way across a big scary ocean. Did anybody ever try to find us? Find me? Lizzie's mother and father probably don't want to see Papa after he took their child away."

#

Johnny is adept at inner speech, where quiet thoughts flower in internal expression and creativity blooms into outside voice. Or is stymied with sorrow. But optimism remains the theme, the never-breaking thread to survival, even with daily struggles and many questions unanswered. He just marches on: a young boy with so little in his life stays rich in his faith.

With only one or two, maybe three, years of exposure to rudimentary Catholic conscience, no longer available after arrival in Coney Island, Johnny still carries the familiar rhythm of catechism in his heart. He doesn't want Mary and Jesus to forget him.

Today Papa has gone out to take care of some business without inviting his son. But Johnny doesn't mind: he feels secure that his father will be back, garment and satchel confirming from a corner of the room. And he's preoccupied: quietly sitting cross-legged on his cot, deep in a daydream, eyes distant and sad as he continues to wonder about the grandparents. And Lizzie. He's been thinking a lot about her lately: even her name. He wouldn't have called her by her first name, ever, of course. It is only when he's in private thought. Once in a while he might have used the more formal 'Mother' in reference or reverence, but he doesn't think so. Because he only really remembers her as Mama. Except when he thinks about her as the young girl skating on the lake with Papa. Then she's still Lizzie. Later, in America, when she becomes a mother, then she is Mama. It is an honor to have the name Mother or Mama, Aunt Agi told him a long time ago back home in the big house. "Plus Mama sounds better than Lizzie: no buzz in it," he says, imitating the sound like the child he is.

His father has returned, and after a light meal of Morris cold cuts and bread for both, Frank sips a bit more of his 'spirit' tea and retires. Johnny does not sleep. With insufficient understanding of his parents' departure from a comfortable classical life in Austria to one of insecurity and absence of family in America, he can't articulate his feelings, nor calm the fast beating of his heart.

So he intuitively uses his imagination as a salve: the portraits in his mind come to life in leading roles as Grandma and Grandpa Illar and Grandmother and Grandfather Huszar. They are just now arriving for the family reunion. They have traveled all the way across the ocean and over rugged terrain to meet him, their grandson, at his first home in a little valley town at the bottom of the mountains; and they are so happy to be there. They do a lot of hugging. Even Aunt Roza and Aunt Agi are there to meet his special grandparents. It makes Johnny happy to see his papa and Aunt Roza talking nice to each other again. But the very best thing of all is that Mama is back. As always she's busy in the kitchen fixing something special for supper, and there is happiness and laughter all through the house. And later Uncle Rudi will come with his magic, Johnny decides as he curls up on his cot and slumber slowly steals the scene.

#

Johnny's curious nature is again at play the next morning. Spreading peanut butter on bread past its prime, he offers breakfast to his father. And while Papa eats, Johnny hovers, eager to get going with the storytelling and time travel back home.

"Exactly how did you get over here, Papa?"

"Lizzie decides it all. She says she has plan for us to run away by train, to Paris first, and then to port at Le Havre for steamship to America. I tell her no. I must save money for our passage. She tells me she does not want to wait. She cries. She is so sad. I do not want her to cry. I cannot resist.

"We sneak away from our homes in the middle of the night and when we reach Paris in late afternoon, Lizzie quickly sells all her jewelry for our journey. Valuable stones from her mother and grandmother, heirlooms they are called. I beg against it, but it is done."

"Consider it my dowry," she tells me. "What else are the gems for if not to bring me happiness?"

"And if I am her happiness, if life in America is what she wants, then it is well with me."

The father, not usually an open man, has succumbed to the sweet persuasion of his son, recognizing now how important it is for the boy to learn about his lineage, intending to further share memories and time with him.

"Yes, I will tell you whole story, Johnny, but first we go enjoy outside."

Holding tight to his father's hand, they walk in the soft falling snow, a treat for both. Afternoon hot dogs from the ever-present Abe serve as both lunch and supper. Frank does not suggest French fries, so Johnny stays quiet. He doesn't need them: he's already well acquainted. Early evening brings more questions. Johnny sees his father is tired, but he doesn't want him to be too tired to talk. Instead he will make him extra comfortable.

"Here, Papa, stand up a minute," he says, placing his blanket, folded over once, on the canvas as a mattress, patting it lovingly. Again, his rolled-up sweater makes a soft pillow for Papa's back. "What about the boat trip, Papa? Was it scary? Were there big waves? Did you get seasick?"

"We board as emigrants," he answers. "But first we have medical tests and special baths. Our berths are below in new third class that replaces steerage in most transatlantic ships. Many rich and important people are traveling too, but they are on the first and second-class levels.

"Yes, the waves are big, even monster size when storms come. In winter there are not many calm days. I am one of lucky people that do not get sick from motion. To my sorrow Lizzie suffers seasick all of voyage.

"It is steamship, not boat," father reminds son as he begins to remember how it rolled and vibrated across the sea, a waiting room on water, bound for the enviable first touch of land on America's shore.

And then without explanation, Frank ends the evening. Perhaps reminiscing revived the pain of losing Lizzie. Also, he's been very tired. "We talk more in the morning, my son."

#

"Wake up, Papa; it's a different day," Johnny happily announces while lifting the dust-layered paper shade up toward an early sun. "I have crackers and peanut butter ready. Do you want some honey too? It is from Mrs. Zimmerman."

Frank accepts, sparingly, and his son waits patiently: though his first question for the day is impossible to contain. "So exactly how rough was it, Papa? Were you scared? Did you hide?"

"What do you mean, Johnny?"

"The trip on the boat; I mean the steamship."

"Oh, yes," Frank says hesitatingly, collecting his thoughts. "Yes, that was rough time. But we are on one of just-built ocean liners. It is ship's maiden voyage, just one week after tragic maiden voyage of Titanic. Maiden voyage means ship makes first trip with passengers," he explains. "It is so sad about collision with loss of more than 1,500 people. But I do not fear our travel; I know it will not repeat. Still, I say prayer for good nautical skill of our helmsman: that he knows not to turn too much north where hard-to-see ice hides in the waters.

"Most emigrants, 2,000 or sometimes even more, are in third class now, no more steerage where you are forced together like animals in cage down in bowels of ship. In our France—the name of ship—we have berths of four and six so we do not all live and sleep in open space together; and meals they serve in small food rooms on real dishes. This is not usual way in the third class; we benefit from new ship. We do not need always to stay below either: we are allotted space on a low deck to see the ocean. But Lizzie cannot watch what is making her sick. She clings to me most of time she's awake, holding on to her dream of America. Our hope keeps us alive. You must remember that for your life too, my son: keep faith, educate, and work hard. Always expect to make things better. It is when you feel no promise, no pride, that you fail."

"I will do what you say, Papa. I will not fail. But what happens next for you and Mama?"

"We feel the stormy sea around us, because we are below two levels. I hold Lizzie as still as I can, as long as I can. I keep her warm. And while she sleeps I listen to others talking, and learn from them what they know about America from letters family and friends already living there send back home to them.

"They say not to stay in New York City. It is best to settle in land more like what we know. They tell me they are going to Western Pennsylvania where there are mountains almost like our Alps, with hills and valleys, and thousands and thousands of acres of forest. Maybe like our Vienna woods, I think. One man has brother living there in little village. He says there is very much opportunity for work because it is fast growing railroad town, halfway between cities they call Baltimore and Erie. And Pennsylvania Railroad Company has huge yards where they're building railroad cars and tracks, and that means they need good people to fill all those jobs.

"I decide to follow. It will be good for us. Lizzie is sleeping, but I wake her to tell of our future: 'Everything will be fine now, Lizzie. We are going to make real home near valley in high hills way west of big cities. There will be pastoral land and rugged hillsides with deep forests, yet we are near town of good jobs too. We are going to Pennsylvania! It is where our new friends lead us. And when we get close to the brother's village, we are getting married at the first Catholic Church I see!'

"She smiles so sweet, [sic] but her eyes keep trying to close again. It is wise choice I make to go where families on ship tell me about. They are sure it is like home, but better; and they promise so much opportunity for the skilled and educated," Frank repeats to himself.

"Already they know northwest Pennsylvania at the tip of the Alleghany and Appalachian Mountains is region where they want to settle, like the man's brother did in its valley. They say mountain rivers give best trout fishing, and that ground is fertile for cattle farming and hunting game. They tell me they feel it in their bones. I think I begin to, too. Even before seeing its beauty and bounty, we know the land. Yes, because our centuries-old homeland and this land thrive in archetypal heritage."

#

A haunting question from his son stirs Frank to memories and thoughts, essentially new, that he expected to face only years later. But he shall be true to himself, deep breaths and all. Yes, he will miss his parents, and hopes they do not grieve the separation. He will miss his studies, the libraries and museums; his beloved Alps, the drama of opera, the excellence of symphony, and the perfection of Viennese pastry. However, he leaves with absolute belief that such beauty and sound will forever echo in his soul. It is time now to close the claret drapes of velvet and empty the orchestra pit. It is time that they, he and Lizzie, write their own score on the soil of America, the antithesis of the palatial epicenter of art that is now their past. John can already envision the glory of living in the shade of the majestic mountain range on land lush, hilly, and prolific. They will build a home. They will have children. They will be happy there. He knows that God has a plan for him, and it is good. Right now, though, Frank needs to end the musing. His son is waiting. Ancestry and the making of more is at stake.

"So what happened when you got off the ship, Papa? Did you stay with your friends that told you where it would be good to live? Did you go to the mountains with them? Did Mama get better on land? Did you find a church? Did you marry her there? Right then? How far did you have to go for your job? And where did you go to live? Is it where I lived too? How far away is that? What's the first thing you saw of America?"

"Statue of Liberty," he answers.

"Oh, right, we saw the picture in my book, remember?"

"Yes, and one day I will take you to see her up close, Johnny."

"What else did you see, Papa?"

"We see Ellis Island and lots of people waiting."

"What's fellas aisle?"

"It's where we are detained before we can enter America. There are questions to answer and forms to fill out, papers to sign, and physical exams to know our health. Processing they call it. Oh, and the name is actually Ellis Island, spelled E-l-l-i-s I-s-l-a-n-d.

"That is all for now, my son. It is dark outside and I am needing time for good sleep. I am very tired and cannot go on." Frank turns to a fetal position, his face now against the soft side of the bedroll pillow. He falls asleep almost immediately.

"Good night, Papa." Silence. "Thank you, Papa." Still no reply. Johnny tucks his grey jacket around his father and sits opposite the cot, lovingly looking at the man. It doesn't matter that he's sleeping. He is there. He has given.

Chapter VIII

The father leaves next morning, never waking Johnny to say goodbye. As always, he feels secure in the knowledge his resourceful son will survive. He has paid the rent and placed coins on the makeshift table for emergency and an occasional treat. The air, heavy with stale odors from last night's Coney Island curb cooking, reminds him his son will never go hungry. He has adult friends who look out for him—the Zimmermans, Morris, Abe—and he's such a smart kid he'll be fine. No doubt about it. Frank is convinced he has provided for his son.

In the quiet of that early hour of the father's departure, designed to prevent risk of Johnny seeing him tremble from developing weakness, Frank meets Frank. Soul searching doesn't come easy to the man, but the Johnny effect on his heart has. He has been inspired by his young son to let the love out. Yet he walks away. He has no excuse—his own code of ethics being "nothing is legitimate when it cannot be seen." For example, if he used a cane it would suggest a disability or severe pain that his child could understand and accept, like the need to leave for medical care. But there is no cane, and there is no reason, and now there is no Frank.

He thought it better to leave quietly, hoping that there will be no unkind talk of disinterest, for that is far from the truth. He would never want mistaken words to hurt Johnny, but he's a strong understanding kid and will rationalize an appropriate and optimistic explanation for the exit. He's quite experienced in the task.

#

The question that follows the stealth is not new. But it begs an understanding well beyond expected fiduciary behavior. What force is so compelling that this father is willing to leave such a loving child? Frank hardly knows his son: the surprisingly devout, generously forgiving, and patient little man, virtually unseen by the elder. Johnny even forgives the unforgiveable: cold abandonment. Rejection is raw, unarmed, and personal. It is an insult of highest order, and harmful to a child. At least Johnny has shelter in an attic well above the dank dungeons that house and punish castoffs. Appreciation for his own comfort adds to his ease of pardoning his papa.

That was always true for my father: regardless of those long-lasting dreadful years alone he forgave, would not judge, nor discuss. He held his father in high esteem, faithfully, right up to his last breath, honoring him with absolution and the gift of love. Even after his death, my father was still shielding him.

When I interviewed Duke Fredlund at his home in Sydney, New York, years ago, he remembered that my father had always been reluctant to talk about his father: "He was very protective of the man," Duke said. "Once I asked him if his father had been in the war and he answered, 'No: he had a little medical problem that always held him back,' he said. "He seemed sad talking about him," Duke added. "I felt bad that I asked."

#

We shall never know what the man was thinking when he tiptoed away from Johnny in early morning cover. He'd been increasingly lethargic, not unnoticed by his son. It might be that he is experiencing depression, the realization of time closing in on his opportunities, or, conversely, he may be obsessive about his work and feels guilty for taking a few days off. Or, perhaps, he simply needs to regain self-esteem and pride in respectable employment, where he can use his talent again in ambitious inventions. It could also be the weight of wanting to do more for his son: altruistic intention, preparing and paving a better path for him. Maybe Frank just doesn't think much about time. The 'later' mentality that procrastinators and dreamers rely on has a way of finalizing on its own terms.

If Frank is restless and struggling against pain and deterioration or disease, he is not alone: similarly is the battle of his little boy, wandering without purpose, innocent still, but poised to suffer the disease of the streets. Does Frank ever consider his son alone in long and lonely nights? If a day of work delights a young child, how deep is his dark?

#

Waif: the definition fits. So does truant.

In good weather, Johnny drifts among the vendors and barkers along the midway and beyond. Summer is his favorite season because it allows him to go to the beach anytime he wants, but he only swims within daytime lifeguard hours. The waves are always big. Sometimes he meets nice kids around his age and they play ball and build sand castles. Too often, however, they don't live nearby. John's good looks draw people of all ages to him. His genuine sweet spirit saves him: no one, once they speak with him, would want to do harm, not even the Coney Island predators who are frequently hunting young prey. If anything, they serve as protectors for Johnny. He has become a kind of regular, if not a curiosity, in and around amusements and fast foods. Many workers know his name and they know his need, most of them responding generously. Ray, over at a ticket booth in Steeplechase, sees to it that Johnny rides the junior daredevils once in a while for some fun. And Connie and her brother Eddie frequently 'employ' the boy to clean stalls and set up their games. Johnny covets the spoils of hard work, devotedly collecting his quarters for his coin changer. Mrs. Katz seems always to find an extra cheese blintz or two at her station. She made Johnny her official taster: "Here, honey, sample this one for me today. Tell me, as good as yesterday?"

They are his friends, and he thinks about them a lot. He wonders where they go, what they do when it comes time to close shop. What kind of other life do they have? All he really knows about these kind people is that once the rides stop and the shutters close, they disappear. Abe has started to worry that Johnny is vulnerable with his handsome face and honest charm. He's concerned that certain men and questionable women might begin to flirt with him, introduce him to the wrong things, and try to manipulate his easy-to-trust nature. It's time to have a good talk with the boy.

He's beginning to feel like a father.

Chapter IX

There would be no more visits from Papa. Only after an absence of more than two years did Johnny see his father again. After all the waiting, always knowing in his heart he would one day be reunited with Papa who still loved him and would keep his promise, they are finally together. It fulfills a part of Frank's second promise to Johnny, the first being the coin changer: the second, the vow: that Papa for sure will always come back for his son in Coney Island. Instead their reunion takes place much later in a dimly lit hospital room at the eastern end of Long Island. It is brief, and it is sad: mere moments of touch. The life Johnny once knew, and the poverty he did not, has ended.

#

The theft that my father first sensed, but needed to deny to himself at so young an age, occurred during his residency at the Herriman Farm School when he was about nine or ten years old. By masterful manipulation, he was robbed of precious hours, even days, of essential bedside conversation with his father because a person in the Herriman headmaster office had quietly discarded the Western Union telegram requesting that Johnny immediately be escorted to the Eastern Long Island Hospital where his father lay critically ill, calling for his son. Whether the recipient ignored the importance of the message because of the inconvenience it predicted, or the budget adjustment it might require, or even worse, a cold heart ruling another's destiny, the message never reached the right eyes. There was a second message, identified as such, emphasizing immediate response: FATHER DYING. CALLING FOR SON. ESCORT MASTER JOHN HUSZAR TO EASTERN LONG ISLAND HOSPITAL, GREENPORT. DIRE.

Johnny boards the next train.

#

The identity of the offender who withheld the first Western Union telegram was obvious but never admitted. The belief is the headmaster's wife was at fault, that she did not deliberately intend to do harm to Johnny and his father, but was led by her fear of loss. If Johnny were to learn the location of his family members in Pennsylvania with legitimate rights of guardianship, at his father's death he would be taken from her and returned to them. She knew that. Or if a proper search of Pennsylvania records was to be conducted, and achieve success in finding a family member, there is no doubt he would be returned to his roots. She knew that too. And Margaret Eckard would be devastated. She had grown to love Johnny as deeply as her biological children. Because of a heart murmur he lived in the headmaster farmhouse rather than the cottages the other boys called home. A close family bond became Margaret's joy. Apparently her husband's as well, for when years later he received a letter from my grandfather, Alfred Castle of Inwood, Long Island, requesting a reference in regard to my father's worthiness to marry his daughter since he had no family history behind him, the response was glowing. And at the end of all the words of praise, Mr. Eckard shared a lingering sorrow: he wrote that it had been his parental responsibility to educate his own biological children, Margaret and Stephen, but that John had genius in him and he was the one he should have sent to college. "I wholeheartedly recommend John to you. You and your family will be honored, not diminished, by his addition. He will be a blessing."

"Very truly yours,"
Baynard Eckard, Headmaster

#

At the time of his second promise to his son, Frank had already sensed his impending decline, and with severed family ties had turned to Saul and Rachel Zimmerman for help. He engages them on their front porch early the morning he walks away from his son. "Yes, we will check on Johnny each day, and I will make sure he has good food," Rachel offers. "And when I say good food, I do not mean what comes from the Coney Island griddles. And yes, I will accept some money now for his appetite and laundry, and expect more by mail as we go along. Though he seems to eat little, and I will only have to scrub his clothes on my board occasionally. A little boy doesn't care about clothes. But this can't be long term: we have our own children to consider. So you go get things together—your work, your life—and come back for Johnny as soon as possible. He needs to be in school! He will fall behind; I think maybe at least two grades, or three. Yet already he's very smart: how this is, I don't know. But this I do: he has to learn the right lessons from a real school— the public, Catholic, or Jewish. I know no others in Brooklyn. Saul lets his wife do all the talking, as is customary, but his face says plenty. Frank thanks them both and hurries away.

To where, no one knows. The attentiveness of his neighbors is noticeable to Johnny, and appreciated. Somewhere deep in his soul he understands that his life is atypical, but he doesn't want to ask questions. He's just thankful for the visits from Mrs. Zimmerman that regularly include meals and sometimes clean clothes. Even better than that are the times he is invited into her home, inside to eat with the family at a big table, and then to spend time with the older children. Benjamin loves to read and is generous in sharing his books. It is a pleasant way to wait for Papa. One day the mailman hands Johnny a letter with his name on top but with no return address and a smudge over the stamp. He hurries upstairs to read the very first letter of his life.

I had to leave you, my son, for a little longer this time. Your friends, the Zimmermans, have kindly agreed to look after you until I return. When I am finished, we will find another place to live: a better home for you. And you will go to school. I am negotiating now to sell one of my inventions, and soon there will be enough money to do these things. I will make you proud. Your Papa.

The letter seems intended to pacify Johnny but also has the heart of honesty. The man cares. Johnny folds the letter and places it in his treasured Children's Bible. He thinks it's best not to mention it to Mrs. Zimmerman. The weeks were many, well beyond the gracious allowance of time provided by the caring neighbors. They even invited Johnny to live with them a little while, sharing a room with Benjamin; but Rachel, with wisdom and a heavy heart, lifts the burden from her children—never voiced, but revealed in demeanor, and a mother's instinct—of an outsider in their home. Any child is fragile, and Rachel spoke to that when she explained to Johnny, 'the sleeping quarters are a bit too tight up there with Benjamin, and could we go back to your sleeping at home, but still having meals with us? Okay, Johnny? We love you," she adds for good measure. "You understand, don't you?"

"Yes, I do; don't worry. And I guess I'll go up to the room and get my stuff right now if...."

"Of course, go ahead."

Rachel takes a deep breath: that was not easy.

"Bye, thank you," Johnny waves, heading out the side door. She's surprised at how fast he left, and calls out behind him, "I will bring you some soup a little later."

It's unclear if he heard, but she will take her soup and sin over to the boy anyway. Of course, there is no sin: she's just feeling guilt where there is none. She simply did her job: responded to the silent call of her family. But she's still troubled by ongoing responsibility and the fear that she may have deeply hurt Johnny. Did it feel familiar, like another rejection?

#

Knowing that Johnny should be in school and not walking the back streets of a carnival city, Rachel is concerned about the legality of giving him shelter without enrolling him in the local public school, less a violation now that he sleeps again at home, but still uncomfortable for the amount of care they provide. She asks her husband to join her at the dining table.

"Saul, this is no way for such a smart and sensitive little boy to live. It is wasting his time for learning. Have you been trying to find out about his father? He has sent us no money, made no contact, and I get headaches now over this open-ended arrangement. We cannot continue to worry about this child."

"Ah, Rachel, my heart is heavy with concern for this boy too. I do not know what the man does. I have called the precinct, and they do not know anything about the father. But then they tell me we must turn the minor over to some department, of well care I think he said. It must be the charities."

At nine years old Johnny time—remember the extra candle on a birthday cake—he is actually eight and shockingly innocent of his truancy. It was always his desire, a real longing, to attend a school 'as soon as Papa comes back' to enroll him.

"Makes you wonder," Saul says, "about the school system here when it fails to notice at least once over these years a little boy walking around an amusement park alone, even during school hours sometimes." How did they not see? His tone reveals his disgust. "They say maybe he can be in the orphan program, Rachel," and she gasps from across the room where she is folding Johnny's few garments fortuitously washed and hung out to dry. "I have been trying for the best way to tell you. They will come for him soon: in the morning. I mean tomorrow morning."

"Oh, no. Oh no, Saul. No! This is happening too fast. What have we done? Oh, I must go to him. I will take him some chicken soup: he probably only had peanut butter and crackers for supper. I wish I knew this before tonight's meal. I would have asked him in. I've been trying to pace the times we have him share our table. They're not rude to him, but Hannah and Ben only tolerate Johnny being here, though he goes home now like before. Preteens tend to be very proprietary you know. "I must go to him now," she says, "and you will put the twins to bed tonight. It will not be easy to tell this child his life is changing. God be with me."

Rachel is correct in her keen intuition. The older Zimmerman children have had mixed emotions about their mother's project. They like Johnny enough, but he comes too often and stays too long. Especially when a dessert night happens to feature their favorite. Johnny considers them friends anyway. He can feel their resentment, understand it kind of, and forgives. But he never declines an invitation. He delights in the flurry of activity after dinner when the young twins run around the house avoiding bedtime and Hannah practices the piano.

"Don't you need to go home by now?" Hannah asks.

"Yes, I suppose I do. But I like to hear you play. It sounds nice. I want to learn the horn."

"Oh," she says, turning back to Beethoven.

#

Polite and cute won't cure the reality of what Johnny read recently in his history book: the caste system. It caught his attention because he's been so interested in his own heritage and the stories left behind. He already has one—the love story on ice—that Papa told him all about. But that doesn't determine position. He doesn't know yet exactly where he is on that ladder. "How do you find out? I know it's the birth thing, but where did it start? Way past my father and grandfather for sure; maybe even back to a royal prince? Who knows? I could be next in line," Johnny muses, taking a theatrical bow. He loves to laugh. Even to himself.

Actually, my mother used to say that to me. I'd forgotten until just now the many times she attributed a royal possibility to her husband's unknown lineage. She told me that oftentimes my father was assumed to be 'of the rich' or 'possibly royal' simply because of his innate elegance. He certainly was not trying to impress. He was humble and very kind, with absolutely no hint of arrogance. But isn't the intangible thought of a child, replayed a generation later by his wife, a curious connection of two minds?

Both my mother and father had discussed travel to Austria with the goal of finding aging members of his family. They would utilize the university and Rathausmann, a towered Old World architectural building in which document-rich Vienna City Hall resides; and the libraries, of course, for old newspaper articles on file or film; they might even include a try at something 'magical' with walks through glorious gardens and parks of the city, looking for that certain someone with a familiar family face. The idea was exciting, and they came close to final plans and deposits. They bought new luggage, Samsonite's hard-shell in dark green, and two passports. And amid this busy time in their life, bonded always as one, they forgot as one the frailty of a heart. The first attack took my father to the hospital for two weeks with exit warnings not to travel. The second took him away.

He would never know if he'd been saved a place at the palace table but he found fun in the idea of it … the possibility of cousins, maybe a prince and princess to ride horses with far into the royal woods, or to play high games of popular lawn croquet in challenge to the king.

But the contrast of opulence to rootless is cold water clear for Johnny as he remembers that just days ago he lamented his garret an empty echo chamber, and his body floating just above ground, unhinged, and nowhere to land. Not to worry: no need to land because no one is waiting at the gate to take him home. Still a little boy, having just turned eight, Johnny responds to life's punches with grace. Except there are two words he desperately dislikes. He feels that when put together they sound judgmental and hurtful; not always, but even once can stain a heart. The words are "**don't belong**." He would like to banish this double-edged sword. It's too easy to feel the pain, whether it be intentional or by careless conversation. It seems young Johnny has an empathic soul. By birth or experience?

He sees himself as a guest, not a beggar, in the Zimmerman home. And he knows to respect the invisible do-not-disturb sign belonging to Hannah and Ben. Theirs is mercurial acceptance at best. They feel forced to accommodate the 'outsider' when they never even had a chance to discuss it as a family. Nevertheless, this outsider feels fortunate for every invitation he receives from his very kind neighbor. He has found a spoonful of happiness. So when Mrs. Zimmerman tells Johnny he will be going away, his heart sinks. It sounds so ominous, state officials coming for him. He takes the news with his best composure, maturity beyond his years. He reminds himself that, "Neighbors are not family, and it's God's will for the family to come first for everything. I think He made it for the animal kingdom too: They sniff, growl, or snip at outsiders to protect their family first, before they will play. And little birds just hatched have to be guarded first, ahead of others in the nest, so bully birds can't dip down and scoop them up for supper.

"God makes good rules. I get that," Johnny says softly; unheard by Mrs. Zimmerman. He studies her eyes… but for what? Looking for a sign of sadness, or a way to undo a mistake? Well, nothing is there. The eyes are cold, her friendly nature apathetic.

"It has to be done, Johnny. It's the right thing for my family—and for you," she adds. "You need to be in school. Here are your clothes; maybe a little damp so spread them out on one of the cots. And wash up. They will be here in the morning."

"Guess she really didn't like me being around so much either," Johnny begins to believe. "Nobody really did, even though I asked to help any time I was there. When you don't belong, you just don't belong. Like I said.

"It's a good thing thinking is quiet time and private: 'cause it would make Mrs. Zimmerman very sad if she found out her family had hurt anyone. Even me, I think. Probably. 'Cause she wants everybody to be safe and happy." Rachel Zimmerman is just about ready to leave when Johnny says, "Thanks for being so nice to me, Mrs. Zimmerman. You cook real good [sic] and make great cookies. Hope I can say bye to Mr. Zimmerman too. And don't worry, I'll be way ready when they come for me."

She winces at the sound of his words, 'when they come for me.' At least her way of saying the same thing had been less harsh, less institutional. She wanted to cry. Next morning before pickup, Johnny is able to talk with Saul. Rachel had reminded him to take time to go next door and say good-bye before work.

"And good morning for [sic] you," Johnny responds to Saul. "I want to thank you for the fun I had at your house, Mr. Zimmerman." Saul begins to feel the weight of the inquiries he made that set this sorry situation in motion. "You and Mrs. Zimmerman are very nice people, so thank you. I have something to ask you, okay?" Saul's grin is his permission. "So, well, when my papa returns next time, would you please tell him how to find me? I will ask someone to tell you where it is after I know where they are taking me. Okay?" Saul nods in agreement, clears his throat, blinks his watery eyes while biting his lip, and with a goodbye barely audible flees the scene.

#

Only one person from the several curious neighbors gathering on the Zimmerman lawn has dared to show any emotion or voice good luck as Johnny is escorted to the dark official-looking vehicle, and that is Hannah. She took him by surprise as she stepped out of the line and out of character to grab hold of his arm, and looking straight into his eyes she says, "Hope you like it there." Quickly she turns back to join the others and misses the breadth of his smile, evidence of just how much the gesture meant. What Johnny, new ward of the state, does not know as he slides into the backseat is that Rachel Zimmerman has been in full control, that she has prepared herself for the parting of a child. It tears at her nurturing heart to turn the boy away, even knowing it is in his best interest, and not negotiable. She fights hard against any display of emotion, tightens every muscle in her face, and focuses her eyes on an object just beyond the boy she has learned to love. It was difficult but the performance impeccable, making it unlikely Johnny will ever know its truth.

The navy-blue sedan inches away from its limited audience, yielding momentarily before easing into the flow of traffic. At the same time Rachel, watching the blue disappear, yields as well: to a flow of tears, inconsolable now after hiding her grief from Johnny.

#

Routinely, after a hearty brunch, a morning walk with the twins is pure joy for Rachel. Also good exercise, and of course, fun for the boys. On the way home from the playground they always stop at the corner store for a treat: today dollops of ice cream in a cup for David and Daniel. This day Rachel doesn't order the usual egg cream, her system still not quite right after the upsetting event of a few days ago. Another daily routine is to pick up the newspaper from the pile just outside the door. She always pays ahead so automatically takes one and folds it, intending to read later when the boys nap. When Saul arrives from the office for a quick lunch, he hears a harrowing scream that causes him to jump the broad cement porch steps two at a time. He finds his wife in the kitchen, her teacup overturned on the table next to the day's newspaper, violently pushing away what she cannot bare to see. He holds her, quiets her, and follows her quivering finger to the face of Johnny, enlarged for the front page of the *New York Daily News*. And there it is, a public plea with the caption, 'Does Anyone Claim This Child?' The text will tell the story, which Rachel will never read, and the handsome boy with the haunting hazel eyes will capture hearts. The hope being one heart belongs to the father.

"My God, my God, what have we done!" Rachel cries. "One more, just one more, what would it have mattered? We could have embraced him as our own. What kind of people have we become?"

Saul tries to calm his wife and remind her of the difficulties associated with adding an unrelated child, of the extra care and cost, and the obligation to educate their own children first. "We know nothing about him really," he says. "Is he healthy? Is he Jewish? Where are his people?"

Rachel wipes first her eyes, then her apron, and picks up the paper she first avoided so she can wave it annoyingly in front of Saul. "You ask such questions like he is dangerous, someone to fear or something. He is a young child for goodness' sake. What's dangerous is if someone answers the newspaper pretending to be a relative or guardian of Johnny and kidnaps him. His father could come back and blame us.

"We are six people living in this house, four of whom should have welcomed Johnny better, made him more a part of our family, living here with us, but no, we sent him away. God forgive us."

Chapter X

The facility on Schermerhorn Street is crowded and clinical, and the overwhelmed young applicant awaits his rescue: "Papa will know and come for me very soon," of this he feels certain. Meanwhile, he looks for a friendly face among the many, but there is none. People are working hard he can tell, and others are sitting on benches or wooden chairs without pillows waiting for their number to be called. He is in a hard chair too, his legs swinging, unable to touch the floor. They didn't call his number: a nice lady took his hand instead, guiding him away from the noise of the main room to her office. She asks him to sit down, walks around to her desk, and leaning across it, says softly: "My name is Mrs. Rupley and I am going to be your representative. Anything you need goes through me, so I can be sure you are well cared for. If you have questions, or feel a little lonely at first, just come to see me."

"Okay, thank you," Johnny says. "But I don't think I will be here very long; I have a father, you know."

"Yes, I do know that and I'm sure he is a very fine man. He will want us to take good care of his son while he is away, and we will not disappoint him."

Johnny smiles in agreement, but his attention has moved to her funny-looking glasses that keep sliding down her nose. He watches them travel down and be pushed back up, never staying up very long as she alternates between writing and repositioning. Unaware of what he found so entertaining, Mrs. Rupley methodically extracts as much information as possible. The answers are incomplete: "No I don't have a birth certificate. No, no health records. I'm never sick. No, I haven't been in school." She compliments his knowledge. "Thank you, I like to read. No not exactly, but it's in the summer. I had a party once. Well, he is American and we lived out in the country near mountains before Coney Island, and there were lots of railroads. I don't remember too much; I turned six at my party. Yes, Uncle, um, um, Rudi, that's right; he's a magician; I remember that. And my aunts were there a lot. Aunt Agi and…."

"You mean Maggie?" Mrs. Rupley asks specifically since it is her job to trace every possible lead to a family member.

"No, her name is Aunt Agi. It's funny, but that's who she is. And another aunt is very nice like my mother and her name is, um…."

"Okay, Johnny, don't fret; you've been very helpful. Let's continue. Did you bring enough clothes?"

"Aunt Roza! That's who is my other aunt."

"Well, good, I'll write that down. But what about the clothes?"

"I don't know. What I have is underwear and shorts, tee shirt, this shirt and knickers I have on now; a sweater and a jacket for when it's cold. I can't remember any more. But best of anything I have in the whole world is my coin changer. I wouldn't forget that. It's shiny like the kind that the ice cream men on trucks have. You know, with a spring and when you press down on the lever, pop, the coin comes out and a little bell rings. Right now I know it contains my 85 cents: three of my quarters and two nickels. I know my quarters exactly because I earned them working at Miss Connie's games concession."

Mrs. Rupley takes a deep breath after such a surprise. Child labor? Oh, dear. Abruptly she stands up to tuck her white blouse further inside the navy skirt and then attempts to smooth out its wrinkles, wiggling back into her chair and sitting up straight into a proper posture, as if fastidiousness, the antithesis of everything Coney Island, might cancel out that confession. She is a purist at heart, very detailed, and already wondering if she should report to her superior that Johnny had been receiving pay for work on the midway of Coney Island where adults and sometimes their children, even teens alone, would pay money to play games to win prizes. Should she look into it? What would it accomplish now? The danger is over. There is no need for punishment: the motive was honest work, just a few years too soon. His desire to work was understandable, even so young. The blame would be on the workers and owners, entirely out of her hands. No, unlike Pandora's curiosity, she will keep this box closed. "And I would like it back now," Johnny is saying, "along with my clothes."

"What—what did you say?" Mrs. Rupley asks. Her usually quick mind is readjusting from too much thinking outside the task of taking inventory.

"Oh, of course, yes, you were asking for your coin changer. I certainly can make sure it is safe and that it will be returned to you when you leave the Children's Aid Society."

"What do you mean? Why can't I have my coin changer with my clothes?"

"Well, Johnny, your clothes are a necessity, a personal requirement. A coin changer is an accessory, something in a different category and not germane to your life here with us."

"What? What do you mean? What's that word," he asks.

"It means not relevant, not necessary at this time," she answers, sounding a bit testy.

"But it is very necessary," Johnny insists. "It's my very own, from my papa, because he wants me to have it. He gave it to me. It's not fair for you to take it away," he says, trying to hold back tears.

Of course Mrs. Rupley understands: it is his teddy bear, his security blanket, a little piece of Papa. She doesn't want him to be in additional distress over it, so tables the subject for later in the week hoping time will assuage his fear of another loss. "Okay, let's put it aside right now and finish our work. Then you can get settled in the dormitory and meet some of the other children. Well, actually, I think maybe we have finished with the intake, Johnny. Just sit here a few minutes longer while I go find one of the assistants to show you around and where you will stay." She has decided it would be wise to skip the last question on the form: the one about personal possessions.

"All right, I'll stay here, Mrs. Rupley."

Johnny didn't say anything after that. But he did a lot of thinking later, sitting on the side of his assigned single bed. He felt betrayed by Mrs. Rupley who had told him she was there to help with anything he needed, and then didn't even want to talk anymore about his coin changer. She just didn't understand the true value of his beloved possession. He would have to take care of things himself. There were several workers walking the halls so maybe they could help him find his special coin changer. And, yes, they were willing to take a look around, even into open administrative offices, to help the obviously very worried little boy. No luck though.

"We're really sorry, big guy; couldn't find it anywhere," the helpers said. "And we looked hard all over the place. But you bet we'll keep on it."

"Okay. Thanks, really," Johnny says.

As they walked away, another kind employee who overheard the problem tries to offer a solution:

"Here, take these 85 cents," he says, extending his hand to Johnny with a big smile of happy resolution. "Go ahead, it's what you came with; it's what's yours. I give it to you as a gift."

"Thank you for being so nice, Mister. But no, I can't: They aren't my 85 cents. Mine are in my coin changer and they won't give it back until my papa comes for me. Your coins belong to you. I only want the ones that belong to me. I want my coin changer, and my money in it!" He is almost in tears. His sensitive side tells him he's beginning to sound rude. He doesn't mean to be, and he's sad to think he may have hurt somebody's feelings. But his other side says it's not rude: it's right to refuse to take something that you know isn't yours. He wants to be fair. This generous man is offering his very own money, and that's not really very fair to him. He's here working for money, and he shouldn't have to give part of his wages away, Johnny believes. "So I really can't accept your money, sir, because I am not going to give up getting my coin changer back with the very same coins I put in there. But thank you for being so nice to want to share your money."

"Sure thing. Good luck, kid," says the worker.

#

Usual procedure is to retain children in the residential wing of the Brooklyn headquarters a couple of weeks, temporarily housing them while exploring avenues that might avoid the expense of placement if alternative protection can be arranged. In this case, they're waiting for a possible newspaper response and return of the child to his father.

Dormitory life and the restrictions of the shelter with only a limited playground are confining to Johnny after the liberty he has lived. And he misses Mr. Abe a lot. Morris too.

"I pray Mr. or Mrs. Zimmerman will be home when Papa returns. They can tell him how to get here to Schermerhorn Street. I memorized it: it's easy 'cause it ends with a horn. And the first part sounds a lot like skirmish, what Mr. Abe showed me over at the old field where men can still play ball, or hang around for fun. So I put skirm first, but spell it right, s c h e r m; then I fit in 'er' in the middle, and last I add the horn." Johnny has just finished when Mrs. Rupley, having stood outside the door to the dorm and heard the adorable soliloquy, approaches him and probably out of character for her, embraces the little boy. "It's so good to see you. I'm sorry I've been busy this week and didn't have time to look for you. But you didn't come to my office so I assumed everything was fine. Did you make any friends?"

"Yes, I played ball and marbles with some of the guys, and then we built a fort. It was fun."

"Well, good, I'm glad. Did you know that today is Friday?"

"Yes, I read the paper."

"Oh yes, I forgot you have been teaching yourself to read. I'm really proud of you, you know."

Johnny half smiled and looked down at his feet, embarrassed by the unexpected compliment.

"Thanks, Mrs. Rupley," he said nearly under his breath.

"So what I wanted to tell you when I asked if you knew it's Friday is that Friday is Popcorn Day at the Schermerhorn Street building."

"That's great; I didn't know."

His dissatisfaction with Mrs. Rupley earlier in the week, the betrayal he felt, and the urgency of reclaiming his coin changer is lifted by the pleasant aroma of the moment. But the delicate subject is not forgotten. "First," says Mrs. Rupley, "let's go over there and sit in those chairs by the window. I have some good news for you. No, don't get so excited: it's not about your father. We haven't heard from him yet."

"Do you think he saw my picture?"

"Oh, dear, I didn't realize you knew of it being published."

"I read the paper. I couldn't miss my face on the front of it. So what do you really think?"

"I think your father might be working somewhere outside the limits of our newspaper routes and hasn't seen that issue. It's only published in metropolitan New York and not available very far out from the city. Your father loves you, Johnny. Sometimes a father or mother has to go away on business or for other reasons, but if there is love, they always come back. And I know your father loves you very much," she says gently, hopefully.

"Thank you for saying that; I know you're trying to be nice, but how can you really know my father?"

"Because I know how much you love him, and you could only have learned that from a loving father. So let's talk about my news now, and then we'll partake of the Friday treat." Mrs. Rupley isn't new at her job, but this case is rare in its revolving-door abandonment. It has been an emotional rollercoaster for the child, and his plight tugs at her heart. She will have to begin her conversation about the accelerated transfer to Upstate with something positive. "Johnny, I just learned today that you are going to be able to go up to the beautiful part of New York State with all its wonder sooner than you thought. It was decided that it will be best for you to be in school instead of idle another week or two."

"But what if…."

"Don't worry, we will stay on alert for any messages from or about your father.

He smiles at her with relief.

"Do you remember the other day when you had your checkup with our nurse?"

"Yes, ma'am."

"Well, she has suggested that you live in the big house with the headmaster and his family instead of one of the cottages that the other boys have to share. You will like the warm comfort of having a bedroom of your own, yet not really feeling alone with all members of the family upstairs, and nearby.

"Mr. and Mrs. Eckard are lovely people," Mrs. Rupley says. "They have a son, Stephen, and their daughter, Margaret, likes to be called Peg. They're near your age, especially Stephen. It should be fun. I have heard they're eager for your arrival. They have heard good things about you, Johnny.

"And it's so beautiful up there. Nature's artistry is at its best in acres and acres of rich farmland and wooded forests right there on the Herriman property."

"That's a given: forests ARE the woods," Johnny wants to say but minds his manners.

"There's a lake for swimming, boating, sailing, fishing, and then a great ice skating season. All kinds of animals make their home there, but mostly the cows: lots of cows, sixty or more. And why do you think so many cows live there, Johnny? Take a guess. Come on. Why?"

"I don't know," he says. Unimpressed by persuasion, wishing he could stay at Schermerhorn a little longer so it would be easier for his father to find him, he doesn't really care. "A cow is just a cow. Moving far from home is a big deal and very scary," he would like to remind her but of course cannot. Or should not.

"You're smart, Johnny," his advocate provokes, "figure it out. Why are there so many cows do you think?"

"Because it's a dairy farm." He thought about calling it a 'dumb dairy farm,' but that would be rude and not in his character. A scream could convey his message. He won't do that either, but he wishes she would just stop talking. Mrs. Rupley senses hidden anger and frustration in Johnny's answer and at first it surprises her; then again, not really. So much to process, everything so new: another move to an unknown place and a new family is, of course, confusing and frightening for a child. Even adults would be affected.

But before Mrs. Rupley can apply her soft side voice to the wound, Johnny expresses his real grievance.

"Mrs. Rupley, you told me if I needed you you would be there to help me. Well, what did you do about my coin changer? Your office is where I left it, so why isn't it there? Maybe it still is there, but you're not looking for it for me."

"No, honey, I mean Johnny, even if it were to still be in my office, I couldn't allow you to retain it. It is not to be in your possession. That's not my rule, it's the board of directors having to follow the state's rule, and we must obey."

"It's not a gun. It can't hurt anybody. It's just plain silly. Well, then, I want to see my coin changer and walk with it to where it will stay until I leave for good. So, can we please go back to look hard once more in your office, and if it's not there, then go to see where it will wait for me? We could go to your office right now to see if it's still there. I don't care if I miss popcorn day."

Mrs. Rupley is adamant. "No, we will not go to my office now because your coin changer is no longer in there. It is with your file, safely stored in a special room that's just for important resident information and belongings; and I assure you they have already applied a tag or label to the coin changer for identification." She extends her hand. He acquiesces.

Together they walk to the promised Friday treat.

#

Mrs. Rupley works Monday through Friday, and the hour is late. With the coin changer subject at rest, she and Johnny are enjoying easy conversation, nothing heavier than melted butter on popcorn. Before she has to leave, Johnny apologizes. She knows she should too, but he's a kid and won't expect one. "I'm sorry for getting grumpy about the dairy farm, Mrs. Rupley. I hope you will forgive me. If we would have time, I'd like to know more about it, the farm I mean; but I think you will be going home soon."

"Yes, I accept your apology, of course, Johnny. Thank you. I understand the pressure that goes along with change, and you've had a lot of that lately. I'm just glad our misunderstanding has been resolved. I really care about you and want you to be happy. You'll start school on Monday, and I know you will love it because your mind is so thirsty to learn."

Johnny swallows his giggles, but the image of pouring a pitcher full of liquid knowledge over one's head will stay with him for a long while. He's still smiling as he asks, "Would you like me to send you a postcard from the Herriman farm, Mrs. Rupley?"

"Absolutely! That's a wonderful idea."

"Okay, I will. Are you leaving now?"

"No, I still have a little time," she says. "We don't have to say goodbye yet. I will be back on Sunday after church to help you with your move, to introduce you to the young men that serve as drivers between Wave Crest in Far Rockaway, Herriman upstate, and our headquarters here on Schermerhorn Street. They are good guys, and you will have fun on the trip up to your new home."

"I guess," Johnny says. "But it's not my home. And it's not for long: just a way to be in school while waiting for my father to return," he reiterates to confirm their 'understanding.'

"Of course, Johnny, we all know that, and we've already put instructions on paper to give to everyone here at Schermerhorn and up at Herriman, so that they all know what to do if they hear from or about your father. They are to notify me, or Major Macy, or anyone on duty, right away. Then we will take care of the rest."

"Good. That'll work. Thank you, Mrs. Rupley."

"You're welcome, Johnny. I want to say that I hope you will realize, and be excited by, this wonderful opportunity that provides a good education and companionship. While you wait for your father, of course. Think about the fun of exploration, outside games to play, animal friends to enjoy, maybe even milk some cows. I've never been on a dairy farm, but this much I know: if you take care of your cows, they take care of you. Calves replenish the herd with manure that feeds the soil that grows food for the herd that produces the milk. Nature's natural cycle. You can be close to the earth up there with the root vegetable gardens, digging delicious potatoes for supper for example, or tending the orchards, picking grapes...."

"Oh, I had lots of them back at my first house. I love them."

"See, and you will also love living at Herriman, I promise. You will meet a lot of friends, some who will become like brothers to you. You'll have great times together. The famous and mighty Hudson River is not far from the property," she adds. "In fact, you will see it at your right much of the way up. I wish you would let me say 'much of the way home' instead, because that's what Herriman will become."

"No, thank you."

"Okay. I understand, Johnny." But still she continues her pep talk: "It will feel familiar to you, living so close to the mountains with pristine lakes and lush forests. Bear Mountain is not far away; and going north takes you deep into the alcoves of the Adirondack Park and along the shore of Lake Champlain. It ends at the junction, very near the Canadian border in the town of Champlain."

"My Papa is from the mountains of Austria, did you know?"

"No, not exactly. You told me you had lived near the mountains, and I just assumed they were more local. I wasn't informed about your father's background."

"He has a lot of background. And his mountains are the Alps."

"Wow," she says. "He sounds very interesting. I'd like to hear more about him someday. I hope to visit you after you've settled in at the farm. Right now, or at least soon, I must to go to my office and put things away before I leave. You know you have only two nights left to sleep in the dorm, which I suspect pleases you. As I said, I'll be here to send you off on Sunday." The sound of 'send you off' bothers Mrs. Rupley: she shouldn't have said it quite that way. It rings of discard. And she fears Johnny hears it that way too. So far he has done well accepting the idea of further change, but he will be unhappy watching the miles adding distance between him and his father. Because even with the lack of dependable love and the unthinkable empty hours without his father, Johnny still has a very strong attachment to the man. It is that bond he holds so dear that causes him to cower against the will of strangers threatening to take him away from his home, his roots, his *raison d'etre*.

"You know, Mrs. Rupley, I was really hoping this next week would be when Papa hears about my picture and hurries home, and then finds out I'm here and comes for me. Now I will be so much more far away."

All of a sudden Mrs. Rupley knows what to do. It came to her out of nowhere. Not really a voice, but a whisper, audible vapor. A **message** Heaven sent? Ew, that brings her face to face with herself, and she's not proud of the mirror image. It has been a succession of intentions but never quite getting there for so many Sundays. This one she's sure about: she told the child she would arrive after church. To fail the commitment is to fail the **invitation**. In fact, she believes this opportunity is divine, the impetus for her surprise in-the-moment-vow to go back to God. Now her saving grace idea actually serves two: a practical solution to assuage Johnny's fear of being too far away and a mystical calling for her to explore further faith. She is eager to emphasize good news to Johnny: that their new truck with improved travel safety will help relieve his fear of living too far away for his father to find him.

After attending church service, Mrs. Rupley hurries back to Schermerhorn Street. No sign of any transportation yet, but good: that gives her the quiet time she needs to talk with Johnny. In fact, they walk around the corner to a small luncheonette for sandwiches. Johnny chooses a hot dog.

"I know you've been concerned about the distance to Herriman," she begins, "but I want to tell you why the trip is now better than ever before. By the way, the scenery is breathtaking.

"But this is what I want you to know: a gift to the Brooklyn Children's Aid Society from the estate of a wealthy and prominent New York City financier—that means his job was all about money—has allowed us to purchase a brand-new shiny white Ford truck with a fully closed body that will make transporting children much easier: in fact possible in many cases. Part of its interior is modified to accommodate the needs of crippled children, and it has up-to-the-minute medical equipment for emergencies. It's like a little ambulance."

"So how much difference does it make?" Johnny asks.

"Well, we haven't always had completely closed trucks until now and that prevented many children in iron lungs, double leg braces, and other inhibiting situations from being transferred to Wave Crest Convalescent Home for summers by the beach. It opens up a new world for them. The truck is larger and will hold more passengers, allow safer lifting in and out, be smoother on the road, and much safer with improved mechanical parts. There will be less, if any, problematic breakdowns than those in the older vehicles. All these automotive engineering advancements should quicken overall efficiency including less driving time to destinations.

"I thought you'd like to know that, Johnny," Mrs. Rupley says.

"Yes, thank you."

"And the blessing is huge," she continues, "made by the best of mechanical minds producing products for the handicapped, the many children once held back by insufficient and unsafe vehicles. They can now have a taste of travel. Most of them have never seen the ocean nor known the touch of sand."

"So we can show them. That's good. I like that," Johnny says.

"But about the driving time—do you like that too?" Mrs. Rupley asks. "Do you see what I mean? No chug-chugging on the road. It will be a smoother ride and indeed a faster trip in the new truck. If your father is waiting for you at the Schermerhorn location and the truck is available, up here, you will be driven as fast as is safe back to Brooklyn," Mrs. Rupley is happy to say, looking up to Heaven with a smile and a wink as a thank-you. She had had no idea what to do for him before the **message** came to her. "That's pretty good news, right?" she asks Johnny.

"Yes, ma'am. Will I be riding in the new truck today?"

"Yes, I was told it has already been delivered, inspected, and test-driven," she says.

Johnny pauses to digest it all. "Wow. That man gave a really great present to us. Now lots of children will surely be very happy, don't you think, Mrs. Rupley? Too bad we can't thank him cause he's already dead, I think. Didn't you say?"

"Yes, Johnny, he's in Heaven now."

"Well, anyway, really, I think it's even better to thank God for the truck since he's the maker of all things. Everything begins with Him," Johnny states with absolute certainty.

"Yes, Johnny, you are so right. Let's pray."

CHAPTER XI

No teddy bear, no security blanket, nothing familiar to snuggle up to as the shiny white truck speeds under ominous skies into Johnny's unknown. He is all bundled up in a pair of corduroys and a long-sleeved sweater, provided by the benevolence of Brooklyn Children's Aid Society, and his still useable grey jacket with a first-time wool scarf around his neck. The drivers, Doug Patterson and Billy Harris, try hard to sound optimistic. Their motto: no gloom and doom talk in an already bleak situation. So it's happy voices and kid questions about pets and friends, school, and favorite ice cream flavor to which Johnny dutifully and politely answers. He's aware of their delicate approach and appreciates their efforts: they're trying to be kind, but his heart hurts. He can't pretend a smile.

Patterson at the wheel, turning halfway around to Johnny right behind him in a little jump seat rather than in back with child-size stretchers and medical equipment, tries to keep up a conversation for the long ride ahead.

"Tell ya' what, big guy, you're gonna find yourself eatin' [sic] some of the best cookin' in the county. Those homemade fruit pies Mrs. Eckard turns out could win ribbons. You'll really like it there. Sometimes I wish I could have the upstate assignment: miles and miles of farmland, beautiful scenery, colorful crops, friendly people, even the animals, and the best milk in town. Next time I see you you'll be telling me how great it is at Herriman Farm School, and then I really won't want to go back to Brooklyn," Patterson says in his best upbeat voice.

He continues the introductory chitchat, expanding where he can. "You probably know, Johnny, that the farm and the school sit on Herriman property; a real pastoral scene of rolling hills, ponds with trout jumping; lakes for swimming and deeper fishing, sledding; animals grazing, sugar maples protecting and providing plush berries and other fruits of the field that together give us a glimpse of paradise."

"But Mr. Patterson, what about the cows? You didn't say them on your list. And they're very important for the dairy business, you know," he says for fun. "No milk to sell without them," he finishes in a hint of sing-song.

"Yes, you are delightfully right, Johnny. But actually I was including the cows when I spoke of 'animals grazing.' They definitely are important and should have been mentioned separately. We can always count on our milk: fresh and on time. Our cows keep us healthy."

"Are kids allowed to ride the horses, Mr. Patterson? I hope so. I've always liked cowboys. One year my mother put cowboys and Indians on top of my birthday cake. It looked real nice. But you can't eat the decorations."

"Yes, of course, you may ride the horses, Johnny. In fact, when the Eckards formally give you permission they will say, 'Not only do you get to ride the horse, you get to groom it too.'"

Double smiles: Patterson and the little boy in the back, both knowing that there's hard work hidden in the hide.

"Don't forget to tell him about the beach," Harris says.

"I was just gonna [sic] do that," Doug says. "The Brooklyn Children's Aid Society has a hospital for crippled children down in Far Rockaway along the ocean for soothing healthful time in the sun. It doesn't look like a hospital because they're separate houses on spacious lawns with shade trees that go almost down to the white sandy beach.

"By the way," he adds," boys and girls can be patients at Wave Crest. But it's only boys up at Herriman. Girls live in supervised boarding homes on Long Island or upstate in country bungalows, or now in Spring Valley, a little town nearby still in its infancy."

"That sounds so funny to say about a town, Mr. Patterson. Don't you think?" Johnny asks.

"You know something, it does sound silly now that you point it out," Patterson agrees. "It would be better to say, 'Still not very big' or maybe 'fledging'?"

"No, I don't think so," Johnny says, picturing a little bird learning to fly, and falling. But he's really not listening now. The word *infancy* has reminded him of babies and that makes him think about the Zimmerman twins. Though they're not really babies anymore: they were already walking and funny running in the house when he was there. Outside they have to stay in their stroller. But they don't like that and try to climb out as soon as their mother turns away to talk to a neighbor. But she can tell, and because they're naughty then they have to go back inside to play. He remembers how much he had enjoyed being around them. Hannah too. And now even that has been taken away from him.

"So, as I was saying," continues Patterson, "Summer means Wave Crest for us. We do the driving, Billy and me, back and forth in the hot weather, but also other times when and wherever we're needed: they keep us busy in and out of the three: Herriman in the foothills, Wave Crest at the beach, and Brooklyn Children's Aid Society spread all over the Schermerhorn block."

"Wow, that's a great job you guys have," Johnny says. "Do you get to go to the ocean before you leave Wave Crest? That would make it even a more [sic] better job, swimming in the big Atlantic. I love to swim in the ocean and jump waves. I learned all by myself at Coney Island where the waves are very big, but I always stay near where the lifeguard stand is. I would like to be one myself, except I'm too small right now. But I know I could save somebody if I'm out there swimming and they're sinking.

"And I've been wondering when you're not on a trip or out driving, where does this new truck stay, Mr. Patterson?"

"Headquarters," he answers with a smile, pleased that Johnny is now engaging so well. "We refer to it as Schermerhorn most of the time, the big building and all. It's the name of the street the buildings are on. It takes the city block. You'll be happy to know they've just built a garage for the new truck to keep out of the rain and sometimes snow."

There's a pause in the conversation: Johnny's now thinking about the fun of snow. And maybe learning to ice skate soon … but he doesn't have skates…. Then he turns back toward Patterson to say: "Oh, I am."

"Am what? Are you all right, kid?" Patterson asks.

"Yes. I am happy to know the truck has a garage."

"Oh … I see … well, good … yes…," Patterson says, kindly nodding in agreement.

Sometimes the flavor of young language provides an unexpected moment of delight. And did just then, warming Patterson's heart. He even saw a smile sitting beside him, but Harris would not budge. Patterson's been studying the boy in a subtle way, turning around in a natural gesture to look at him briefly, and he sees that unhappiness has reappeared on his face after those moments of pleasant exchange. Harris and his blunder may be adding to the melancholy, too. Darn him. He's a good guy, a pro at lifting those heavily encumbered patients for transfer, but he's tactless. Like referring to the boys living at Herriman as disadvantaged. Wonder how Johnny feels about a label like that….

"Hey, Johnny, I know they expect us in late afternoon to make sure you can get settled in and be ready for school tomorrow, but we were delayed in departure and I'm hungry; how 'bout you? We can stop to eat if you want. No problem."

"Well, yes, I am a little hungry, Mr. Patterson."

"Billy, you on board with this? It's my treat," Patterson offers.

"Of course. I never turn down food when somebody else is paying," he says, true to his reputation. They stop at a roadside 'home cooking' cottage for the best food this little guy can remember: a big juicy beef patty with gravy, a baked potato with lots of butter, creamed corn, peas, and biscuits. Other than his mother's cooking, of course, yes, she is the best. Patterson feels good inside, not just from a full belly, but for being able to do that for Johnny. Sure he's hard-pressed for money, but it's worth seeing the kid enjoy all that grub. He offers dessert, but Johnny declines even the cherry topped cheesecake that tempts him from a glass counter display. Patterson doesn't take "No" for an answer—he has seen Johnny eyeing the desserts and persists but the boy still refuses.

"Well, if you won't, I will," announces Billy.

"Good ole' Harris, of course he will," Patterson says under his breath as he mentally tallies and borrows from budget to accommodate his unexpected splurge that now includes the Billy Harris cheesecake. Johnny suspects this nice man is being too generous, which is why he had to say no to his all-time favorite sweet. He recognizes that face of fear: same as his father when it was time to go to Morris.

They're making good time with the new truck, and Patterson is glad he suggested the stop. Actually he's enjoying time with this child. "He's not a typical kid. This one is smart, sensitive, good listener, and respectful. Seems to really want to learn: like when Billy and me are [sic] talking baseball at the table and Johnny asks for statistics: he wants the whole picture. Nope, this is no ordinary kid," he says, only to himself.

Quite frankly, the bold and brawny young man has been touched, not only by the sadness he sees but by the raw quality of this little person. So when Harris breaks the silence and begins a commentary on the rules and regulations for a new resident of a Brooklyn Aid Society home, Patterson has an overpowering urge to lean over and give him a punch. He counts instead. The commandments given, the men now resume sports talk and Johnny listens in. He likes what he hears: he thinks maybe he will play that baseball game when he grows up. Then he curls up for a nap, but before falling asleep hears Patterson, who has pulled over and relinquished the steering wheel to his partner, say very nice things about him.

"Maybe because he feels sorry for me, disadvantaged and all," Johnny thinks sarcastically and silently. He certainly doesn't consider the remark made by Mr. Harris to be true.

"So what do you think about this one, Harris?" Patterson asks and answers. "Remarkable kid, right? I mean all he's been through already. I'm impressed. He's bright and has good manners: he'll do fine at Herriman. Don't you agree, Billy?"

Less animated, Harris agrees. "Yeah, he'll be okay; probably take to farm life like a duck to water."

Testing to see if the boy is sleeping, Patterson says, "Yes, of course he will. You agree, right, Johnny? Are you even awake back there, kid?" He leans over to see him, difficult in the snow-filled darkening sky.

"Yes, sir, I'm awake."

"Oh, don't call me sir."

"Okay. Mr. Patterson. And I hope so."

"Hope what?"

"That I can fit in like a duck to water." There it is again. "I plan to work really hard on the farm and hard on my school studies, too, while I'm at Herriman. But you see, I do have a father and he will be coming for me soon."

"Good for you, then," Patterson says. "I'm glad." And the compassionate student social worker assigned this delivery is truly sincere in his hope the father will show; but he's read the file, seen the newspaper, and knows that as of today's date there's been no response to the bold appeal playing page one. In his college work and Schermerhorn experience, Patterson has seen a lot and is fully aware that once a parent disappears for more than a night out on a bender, the possibility of reunion is much reduced. So he's motivated to protect his little charge from further hurt and disappointment or at least soften the pain. He's still annoyed with Harris for such an unkind thoughtless comment, but keeps the dialog friendly, to help raise John's spirit. He puts his anger on hold until the drive back. Indeed, that derogatory word was impetus for his speaking so approvingly of Johnny to Billy within earshot of the child. He couldn't erase the word *disadvantaged* or pull it from the sky but he could override it with language designed to praise and perhaps forget.

So Doug talks glowingly, with never a hint of the earlier ugly remark, using instead positive words related to advantage: a reference to Johnny's advantage in intellect and skill already evident in his youth. Johnny has had some rough losses in his formative years; none of his own making, of course, so there can be no blame. It is still a life of innocence and promise. *But when it comes, and it does, **the betrayal**, will it damage forever his ability to hope? Can Johnny forgive the unthinkable theft, the trauma of its imagery, and the selfish deceit planned by the person he trusted most? It is incomparable, far beyond anything one could imagine. And yet the horror happens. Johnny is still young, prepubescent, when it stirs. Although the genesis of the crime dates back to his arrival at Herriman about three years earlier. It wasn't planned. It was organic, gradual, and bonding. Unnoticed, especially by members of the newly knitted Eckard family of five, was the increasing attention to, and possessiveness of, Johnny that the headmaster's wife assumed. She may not have been aware of her need, as it grew to be, and her indulgence of a child under the guise of goodness. She didn't mean to harm. She simply didn't want to lose. It was that fear that fueled the brewing of evil destined for fullness in a following year.*

*Only in reflection do the signs blink, warning of the tale to be told: the **tragedy of disregard**.*

Had someone been allowed to see the first telegram message, quick-crumpled and hidden deep in an apron pocket, its importance would have been immediately realized, its instructions followed, and precious words delivered in time. But it did not happen that way, and the intended recipient, Johnny, was robbed of critical moments and priceless information.

The white farmhouse comes into view as they ascend the gravel road, and Johnny feels a quickening inside. It's okay to be nervous he reminds himself, but no sense in being really scared. They're just normal jitters. Lots of people get them.

In fact, Patterson feels a similar rustling inside. He's been here many times, so what's with the anxiety.... No, it can't really be the impending good-bye. No way. Well, maybe.

Other than the drive back to Brooklyn, his job is pretty much done: just moments away the child will enter the home, and so must he for presenting documents to be signed and dated, and then, after the usual invite for coffee and something from the oven, he will be back on the road heading home. Simple as that. At first Patterson had been annoyed being tapped again so soon for weekend duty: a special rush assignment they said. Now, in an odd kind of way, he feels it's an honor.

Johnny focuses on the house, a double-decker clapboard structure, as the truck slows to a stop. It sure is big. But in this case, big isn't threatening; big looks cozy. He was expecting a building but discovers a home. And as little candles flicker in too many windows to count, he begins to feel they are not unlike a beacon, each one signaling safe harbor. The front door swings open even before he has the chance to peer through the interesting etched glass panes at either side; he is greeted by the friendly faces of Baynard and Margaret Eckard, headmaster and wife, surrogate father and mother, who radiate the warmth their home suggests and begin immediately the protocol of welcoming Johnny.

"We've been waiting and we're so glad you're here," says Mrs. Eckard. She crouches down, eye to eye, tentatively touching his shoulders. The requisite summons to appear for introduction to the latest arrival brings both children downstairs for smiles and quick handshakes and a fast return to their rooms.

In a nod to the drivers, Mrs. Eckard says, "Nice to see you again, Doug, Billy. Just happens there's some warm rhubarb pie waiting for you in the kitchen. Mr. Eckard will make the coffee. I remember you both take coffee. And there's plenty of milk for you, Johnny. Do you like rhubarb pie?"

"I don't know it. But I will like it I'm pretty sure. Thanks, Mrs. Eckard."

"You are most welcome, dear. Now run along with Doug and Billy for a trial taste, and when you finish I will show you around the house and to your room." She walks to the office to complete the transaction, and brings forward a packet of signed permissions that she places on the slender maple stand by the front door.

"A rough trip, guys?" Mr. Eckard asks, spilling coffee grounds all over the slippery oilcloth, even more so now that he attempts conversation and coffee making simultaneously. "I've seen how the traffic picks up on the weekends," he says. "City folk seeking country air, I guess."

"We didn't find traffic too heavy this time," Billy says while cutting himself a wedge of pie. "It was us that added to the delay that already started at Schermerhorn: it was our own choice. Sorry: we stopped for a snack."

"Some snack," grumbles Patterson to himself.

Baynard Eckard wipes up the mess he made measuring coffee. He does not shine in the kitchen. While Johnny enjoys pie and Patterson's storytelling in the formal dining room—high ceiling, rich oak—the headmaster tests his audience of one, and soon feels free to further discuss the child with Harris: "Guess we've got some real hard work cut out for us with this one," he begins. But the coffee's ready, so he pours the miss-measured dark syrup for his guests. "Yes, thank you, we do take cream and sugar," they say without revealing 'only today.'"

Johnny leaves the dining room for a little first floor exploration of his own before a full tour with Mrs. Eckard. He steps outside onto the white porch that appears from his vantage point to be wrapped all around the house. He'll check on it tomorrow. Patterson has returned to the cozy kitchen—red brick fireplace and all—and is surprised as he sits down at the table to find himself stuck in a discussion about Johnny. The headmaster is voicing his concerns to Harris: "He's a wanderer, that one. He's walked all over the Coney Island streets, like a little hobo. Who knows what he may have learned from that underworld? From what we know he's never even been in school, and they say he's already nine."

"Don't forget: it's really eight," Patterson quickly interjects: "He's a good kid, I can tell. And he'll pick things up quickly. He's bright. In fact, I'd guess he's self-taught already to a point at least on the level of, if not above, his age group. We were talking in the car. He told me how he loves books. Someone, an older person he befriended, gave him a big history book of the world and he treasures it. He loves to read it, he says, and I believe that. He's walking proof.

"He also likes to read the daily newspaper whenever he can find a throwaway. He told me that there are places where you can sit and read newspapers and books for free. I didn't get a chance to go farther on the subject because we had just turned into your driveway, but it sounds as though Johnny has discovered the public library. I think he may be brilliant."

#

Under the gentle hand of Mrs. Eckard Johnny is escorted upstairs, climbing slowly, wanting to, but does not, turn around for a glance back. "Here we go: your bedroom, John… I hope you like it. It's a single bed, but it should be comfortable for you. And you have a desk for homework and this small chest of drawers."

Johnny stands still. Stunned. Finally he reacts, "Oh, yes, Mrs. Eckard, I do like it. It's so nice and big and everything. Thank you. Really. Thank you."

"Okay, well, let's see: the lavatory is down the hall to the right. I've laid out a towel and new toothbrush for you. Your little overnight bag is in your bedroom closet, along with a few items of clothing for school, church, and the cold outdoors you will need. I will call you very early in the morning—we all rise with Arthur, the rooster; now don't ask why he's called Arthur, or who chose the name, because nobody fesses up to it."

"Well, maybe," suggests Johnny, "if he's the big shot who wakes everybody up for the day, he's kind of a king on his perch, like a throne. King Arthur of Herriman. I know about King Arthur because he's in my history book. He is British, but nobody is really sure if he was a true king or just a legend. Or rooster," Johnny adds, giggling.

Mrs. Eckard is amused too, and as an educator she's thankful for the breadth of awareness he exhibits. She's already a fan. "We'll have an early breakfast, and then I want to see you in my office to complete your part of the voluminous paperwork, after which we will walk over to the school building and enroll you. There will be a test to determine your class level before I can introduce you to your teacher and classmates. Sound good?"

"Yes, ma'am."

Mrs. Eckard asks if Johnny might still be a little hungry after the late lunch and pie, followed by another piece of pie here, or is he finished for the day?

"Well, no ma'am, I'm not hungry, but thank you." He doesn't correct her by telling her he didn't have pie, or any dessert, at the lunch they had on the road. He feels like it might be bad manners. And he's tired, overtired really; a little bit bewildered or disoriented, like in a semi-state of disbelief. But even though every inch of his body wants to collapse on top of the bed, he has a feeling of being unfinished. Not like needing a bath, or brushing his teeth, but something else.

"Well then, if there's nothing more I can do for you now, Johnny, I will say good night and sleep well. Or would you like me to return and tuck you in after your prayers? No? Okay. I do want to say again that it is our pleasure to welcome you to our home. God bless you." She is about to close the door behind her when….

"Mrs. Eckard, um, may I be allowed to go downstairs for a minute? I would like to say goodbye to…."

"Oh, but of course. I'm sorry. Of course you would," she says.

Patterson wasn't surprised to see them enter the kitchen. The boy had been all but whisked away, leaving this new friend also with a nagging sense of incomplete. Johnny walks first to Harris and offers his hand.

"Thank you, Mr. Harris, and I hope you don't get home too late."

On to Patterson with a special smile: "Thank you too, Mr. Patterson, for the ride and especially for the nice meal I had."

The man takes the little hand with its not-a-bad-grip for a kid and returns the handshake. Then, unexpectedly, without caring about men having to behave manly in the presence of men, Patterson bends down and pulls the child to him for a hug. "Thank you too, my pal. You are a pleasure to know."

Johnny is led away with a new and nice feeling of serenity, a comfort so long forgotten. Mrs. Eckard joins Doug and Billy at the bottom of the stairs before they head out: she wants to say good-bye of course but also to personally place the important packet in their care. Doug accepts. Then, just before slipping into the driver's seat, he tells Harris that he has forgotten something and will be right back, as he heads toward the house. "You go on, get the van started; I won't be long."

Mr. Eckard is surprised to find himself face to face with Patterson again.

"Van won't start?"

"Oh no, it's fine. It's just that I'd like to speak to Johnny again, if you don't mind." And so Mr. Eckard calls Mrs. Eckard, and she calls the boy. Quickly, in hand-me-down brand pajamas a little too cute for his taste, Johnny appears at the top of the stairs, puzzled by his friend's return.

"I just want to say, well I mean, look, you might want … might need, to check on something sometime and I thought I should remind you Doug Patterson's the name. I'm usually in the office or the van, or sometimes doing homework there at night, but you can always call and ask somebody to find me, and I will get in touch with you as soon as I can. It's the Brooklyn Children's Aid Society: remember that. And Mr. Eckard here, he has the number. Right? You can get it from him?" Eckard nods approval. Johnny waves good night. Patterson, alongside Eckard, walks to the front door.

"You're not goin' soft on me, are ya ole boy?" teases the older man as he ushers the younger onto the porch.

Patterson clears his throat first: "Must be that darn sinus." And then his answer: "No, not goin' soft at all. It's just that you've got yourselves a special one here, Baynard, if I may call you that. I've already been with Johnny long enough to know when I see it. So will you.

"Good night, sir," he continues. "And thank you and the missus for your hospitality."

She has gone upstairs but calls down to him, "Thanks for the delivery. Safe travel back."

It's very late, but there won't be many people on the road at this hour. The guys know inch by inch the long path home: the food and pit stops, and where to bunk for a few dollars if exhaustion takes over. They know the pro games they want to dissect. They know the songs they want to hear. They've driven this cushy 'one-way single rider' assignment many times. With no heavy lifting, it's almost always an easy gig. Not so much tonight though. It's already feeling and looking lonely in the new truck, made that way by the emptiness left in a little boy's seat.

#

After standing by his window, sans candle, wondering where Arthur might be at this very moment, and how far the fields extend, and where is the barn, Johnny climbs into his bed of luxury, snuggling under big white sheets that feel like silk.

His long day lingers in thought: all the nice people, the enormity of everything new, dreading first-day-at-school fame, and what to say in his nightly prayer. He has to be honest, so he can't say he's thankful to be so far away up here. But he can say in truth, "Dear God, thank you for this nice place to stay, and for Papa." He pulls the down-filled powder-puff pillow up over his head.

Chapter XII

The early years still hurt. Although Mrs. Rupley's prediction that Johnny would assimilate well, and eventually embrace the bucolic life, was correct, he continues to suffer a private pain of loneliness. The pit in your stomach kind. Even so, he fits right in with the brotherhood population and is adored by the Eckard family, partly for his work ethic: readiness and perfection. Partly for his spirit: kind and honest. His reputation with them also includes his best friend, though not competitively: The Eckard family mantra is, "When we need something fixed or built in a hurry, we choose Duke. If we want quality and creativity, we call Johnny." Their roles at The Farm, as it is informally known, rarely overlap. Duke is in perfect health. Johnny is challenged by the heart murmur. But they're good buddies and each enjoys his outdoor work: hard labor for Duke and the others, dairy duty and animal care for Johnny. His murmur is a thorn in little boy dreams of winning baseball games and other team athletics he once hoped to join. Swimming, however, is an appealing alternative, also therapeutic; and when circumstances and seasons permit, Johnny is seen diving from the old bridge into deep lake waters for dedicated exercises, hoping to heal his heart. And having fun along the way. His daily bike riding is another allowable and extremely beneficial workout right there in nature's own amusement park. It is a vibrant dairy farm covering acres and acres of pastoral beauty and offering prolific gifts from quality stock. The fruits of this rich soil are shared with student residents who also toil in the fields, their teachers, other employees, and local friends. Well known, they provide the best milk for the lowest cost possible as a service to the outside community.

Sunday is visiting day but only after lunch. The boys are expected to attend Sunday school and church in town, or Catholic Mass, a long walk away for the young ones. Johnny has decided to explore Methodist; he likes the Sunday school classes and the way the minister teaches at the pulpit: standing up and down on his tiptoes and moving side to side when he's excited and wants everyone to pay attention. Several residents are not orphans; they are there because their families can no longer afford to care for them. But they visit on Sunday to keep close ties, or maybe satisfy the soul. Regardless, there are always guests, mostly families, many extended, on that day of the week after the boys have had their meal. Several of Johnny's friends have real families: Donny's father is disabled, unable to work, so he comes in his wheelchair at every opportunity. Red has too many brothers and sisters for his mother to raise alone after his daddy drank himself to death, so she put him in Herriman. But she arrives with her other kids almost every weekend, laden with a basket full of goodies from the oven. Butch's mom is all he has, and she came faithfully the first few years. Until she wrote a letter to tell her son she'd married a sailor and was living in Chicago. Joey's grandmother is a familiar face every Sunday, usually accompanied by a cluster of cousins. Paddy seems to have half the Irish Army on duty. And there are more, of course, who receive visitors. Duke, Johnny's best friend, is from a real family with three boys and two girls, but there are no jobs for the father anymore and they had to send Duke to Herriman. They come to visit him a lot, so he doesn't have to miss them.

Johnny sits alone atop the broad steps of the front porch, undaunted, ready again for a Sunday surprise as he watches the cars grow bigger on their way up to the main house on the mound. He stands up as soon as a car door opens and with tummy butterflies that always arrive at that moment, he stretches to see who will step out of the vehicle. He waits to make sure everyone disembarks so he can hold on to hope a little longer.

And then, like so many Sundays unfulfilled, he accepts fact and steadfastly returns the next week to his place on the steps. He stays hopeful by faith and theory. Like today, he's thinking, "Maybe Papa doesn't have a car yet. But he can take a train and walk the rest of the way. That's for sure. And as soon as he is possible [sic], he will. He likes trains a lot."

So Johnny pictures his father walking—no, running—up the driveway right into a hug. Or his aunts, finally learning where he lives, asking his uncle to please drive them—in a fancy 'Model T' no doubt, being a famous magician and all—up to Herriman for his very own visitors. "But I can't go back home with them until Papa can come too." Difficult as it is, Johnny's able to withstand the indignity of repeated empty Sundays because of his optimistic imagination, as used above. Here he places Papa first in the dreamlike images he creates: little snapshots rolling across the tickertape of his mind. Other characters are also based upon real people. He hopes his friends who live far away will decide to surprise him someday. Until then, he'll cast them in his scenes. He misses Mrs. Zimmerman, Ben, Hannah, the twins, and always Mr. Abe and Morris. They, too, play vividly along his moving screen.

Pretend can be a healthy tool. It brings life to memory.

The day never came that anyone visited Johnny. Sometimes he'd sit so long on Sunday that his shoulders would begin to ache, and he'd need to get up and stretch. By then people are starting to leave, and it's getting dark so he feels it's time to abandon his post. He walks over to the animals he loves for the love they give back, thankful for their friendship; and for tonight's forthcoming deli meats and salads, sometimes with sweet giggly Jell-O that he likes so much at Sunday night supper. *Duke Fredlund, Johnny's best friend at The Farm and his employee in later years, told me about the good food during my visit, i.e. interview, long after my father's death and his own nearing. He said not to worry about my dad having experienced any brutality, inferior food, lack of heath care, or anything untoward at Herriman. "It was the antithesis of the poor quality, unsafe orphanages, and institutional residences that were so prominent in that era," he said, adding: "We had white linen tablecloths on our dinner tables every night; white porcelain dishes with an unforgettable skinny red trim, and imitation silver flatware. We said grace before every meal. We were two of the lucky ones: we had it good, and we knew it."*

On Sunday the hot meal is served at noon, before the visitors begin to appear. Most often a preacher comes to say grace and stays through to deliver an exhortation. Sunday school and the music in the 11:00 service are the best things about the week for Johnny. They fortify him and prepare him for possibility: that sitting on the steps might bring joy—his father's arrival—that day, and if not, then maybe next week. "Because you know best, Jesus, and have a different day for Papa to come. And it doesn't need to be a Sunday. Mr. or Mrs. Eckard will let him in anytime, any day he comes to pick me up. For sure."

As those days go by and weeks become months and then a year and then another, Johnny remains unwavering in his expectation of reuniting with his father.

#

Then is the day when waiting for Papa ends. A dark day of shock and hot pain piercing through Johnny's body; of disorientation; of denying in any way possible the echoes of words uninvited. Baynard rehearses a grueling presentation before he calls Johnny to his office. By the time the child arrives the chosen words are forgotten, his script reduced to an empty prop and mnemonics, always a favored friend, unable to help in this fevered situation. It is overwhelming. But he tries. Because it's imperative he succeed. Unfortunately, his opening sentence is a disaster that will travel from euphoria to misery. It begins: "I've called you here, Johnny, because we have just received a telegram...."

And Johnny immediately jumps with joy; he hears nothing beyond six little words and his own thinking, that he really does believe in angels even though unseen. They are our protectors and special helpers for God, answering prayers and making good things happen: like when a telegram arrives. With unbridled excitement the child rules the room: animated and allowing no pause, he leaves the man with the message stunned and unsure of how to move forward.

"Oh, wow, Papa is coming!" Johnny jumps up and down with arms raised, ready to tell the world, with no room for other voices. And he begins to sing, swirling full circle, "Papa is coming; my papa is coming; I have to pack; I have to pack," making another full circle turn to the tune. "He's really coming to get me! I knew it. I always knew he would come back for me. Thank you, God! I bet he's already on his way, so I will get ready. I can hardly believe it. I'm going home with Papa just like I always wanted. And prayed for." He spins around again, almost dancing, so excited, so happy.

Baynard cannot find his way into the moments of glee. He's at a loss for an entrance and any suitable words to lessen the shock. He never anticipated such a reaction from Johnny, and he must, with loving kindness, quickly quiet the boy. The dread of telling him has plagued the headmaster for days—yes, it is several days away from the first telegram— and he regrets succumbing to Margaret's earlier persuasion, hoping now to correct the unnecessary delay by overriding his wife and honoring Johnny with truth and permission to visit his father. The second effort of persuasion that has just failed Margaret was undeniably self-serving as was her first attempt that skillfully sold Baynard on betrayal. Not this time, though. In fact, his current courage portends a turning point in the balance of authority. Like many people, Margaret has fallen in love with the little boy lost, only with her it goes deeper: he has become family, brother, and favored son. No one knows him better: he is hers.

And she worries. What if his father finds him and takes him away? Or if those aunts and uncle learn where he is? Or if a copy of an old issue of the Daily News, dated just right, should surface from an attic or basement, and its reader belatedly responds? These are her fears, everyday enemies. She is alone in her obsession and sinister thought, accompanied only by the secret she hides so well. All those Sundays Johnny sat on the steps waiting for Papa, Margaret Eckard, well aware of his intense longing, was actually praying against him. She had become that selfish. Even more devious is when the first telegram arrived: she read it, stuffed it in her apron pocket, and quickly concocted a rationale to dismiss it. Because she knew she would have to tell Baynard of its arrival. Ready and rehearsed, Margaret began: "I don't understand it, Bay, and I don't like it. Out of the clear blue sky, after almost four years, a suspect telegram saying some man, Frank Huszar, maybe Johnny's father, maybe not, is gravely ill at some hospital way out east on Long Island and to please send the child to them as soon as possible. Just like that!"

She isn't sure she has her husband's full attention but continues. "Think what that will do to Johnny. He's happy now, so much a part of our family. He has practically forgotten the past. Why bring back the pain? Why open Pandora's box?"

"Oh, I don't know, Margaret. Do we have the authority to ignore something so serious, so personal? We have no right to play God."

"But look at the journey involved," she says. "All the way out on Long Island. By himself! Scared. Going to a stranger no less. No, I just don't feel right letting him go, putting him through all that. He's just a child."

And the headmaster caves. "Perhaps you are correct, hon. No telling what we'd be subjecting him to. A fine time for a man to remember his son! Where was he when the boy needed him?"

Margaret loves the anger she sees rising in her husband. She has won. She doesn't consider at what cost. Our universal conscience, that deep down near-the-heart voice of reason, is quick to remind her she has crossed the line, if not legally than morally. Decency has failed her. So she covers her ears and shakes her head like a toddler's best tantrum as she tries to hush the truth. Her husband is surprised and embarrassed by the high drama moment, but his empathic soul encourages forgiveness. However, when her personal conflict begins to show in facial expression, he worries about her emotional state. Perceptive Johnny has already noticed the change. "Is everything okay, Mrs. Eckard? Are you sick?"

"Oh no, dear, just an old lady getting tired, I guess. Can't keep up with things like I used to," she says, brushing the problem away.

Only it didn't go away: a second telegram arrived.

#

The headmaster now stands beside Johnny in his misunderstood joy, trying to gather strength and composure to basically destroy a little boy, to whom he—taking full blame, but secreting it because there is no possible repair—owes an inexcusable and impossible debt. He must be both deliberate and compassionate as he interrupts the gaiety to correct a heartbreaking mistake born of evil.

Thus he raises his voice and insists, "No, no, Johnny, you must wait a minute and let me speak. I want you to calm down, please. You don't understand yet. It's not what you think. It's different from what you've been hoping for. I'm truly sorry. But your father is gravely ill and I….

"Johnny? Do you understand what I'm saying? Do you understand what is happening? Can you hear me, child?"

"Not much," he answers. "You are too far away. I can hardly hear your words, 'cause there's thump, thump, thump in my ears, and my head feels funny. Like it is getting big and will pop open. And everything is turning around. I'm sorry, but I think I'm going to be sick Mr. Eck…."

"Margaret, come quickly," Baynard orders his wife, calling her loudly down the hall so as to be heard in the kitchen. "It's an emergency. I need you in the office right away! Hurry."

Together they lift Johnny onto the settee by the window and revive him. Holding the cold compress still to his forehead, Johnny blinks rapidly and asks what has happened.

"You just passed out, dear, nothing to worry about," Margaret says.

"Why did I pass out? I never did before."

"Well," Baynard answers, "it's because of the shock. I was trying to tell you about something very troubling, and I think your brain subconsciously didn't want to hear, so it shut down in a nonthreatening and compassionate way. It's almost as if it were offering you a chance to prepare a little better. Can you understand that?"

"Yes, I think so. Are you going to tell me the shock now? It's bad about my father, isn't it?"

"Yes, Johnny, it is. I tried to tell you the severity of his condition, but you immediately assumed the best and began to celebrate your father's homecoming based solely on the word 'telegram.' It's understandable, waiting years for a message from Brooklyn announcing your father's return, that you would expect a telegram of good cheer. I just couldn't temper your revelry.

"When I finally caught your attention and spoke of 'gravely ill' in reference to the telegram, it seems, like I just said, your body rejected any further mention of the subject, and that's when you passed out.

"But we need to speak more about this," Baynard continues. "Your father is calling for you; he wants you at his side. You must take the train down to the city where you will board another one for the long ride out to the North Fork of Long Island. Gather together a change of clothes and be downstairs as soon as possible. Mrs. Eckard is making arrangements and will give you instructions, the address, a telephone number for the hospital, and some money. You will be on your own in the city changing tracks for the Long Island train that will be a very boring ride for you, so take some books. You will be met at the Greenport station by someone from the hospital staff. Make sure he or she shows an official badge.

"You can do this, right, Son?"

"Yes, sir, I can do anything for my father. Maybe even make him well again. I took care of him when he came home and got sick one time. And Morris helped. They say that people get better when the ones they love come to visit. So that's me. I love my papa and I will visit. He will get well."

Margaret returns from making the calls, and she has packed for Johnny. A sandwich and lots of chocolate chip cookies are included with his clothes. She does not want him to go. She sold herself to Satan to prevent it. But she has lost her power to the emerging bravery of her husband. Johnny tries to be stoic and keep his emotions to himself. He succeeds at first, but tears have washed his face. What do you say to a child whose spirit is vulnerable, porous to more pain, fighting against a finality he cannot yet accept? How do you glue back the many pieces of a broken heart?

Rhetorical questions, rarely answered. Baynard is eager to be on time for the only train of the day, hopeful that in releasing Johnny into its custody he might receive relief from the high stakes emotion and its aftermath. "Hurry Johnny! I will drive you; come on," Baynard urges.

#

It seems almost a whole day from departure when Johnny finally exits the train and meets the nurse waiting to escort him to the hospital. The ride is short, and when they leave the surfaced road for the mostly hidden driveway, a Victorian building, once a mansion graciously donated by wealthy sisters in 1905, now a hospital, looms large and eerily silhouetted against a storm-threatening sky. Its color appears to be aging original white, with little else in facade until the third level with several turrets topped by tin crowns demanding attention. There's no Patterson for support this time and no family with pleasant faces to greet Johnny with open arms at the door. Instead there is an austere reception alcove and a long, dreary corridor with a peculiar odor and a few old men shuffling along with strange expressions on their faces. They may be in an unfamiliar world now: frightened and powerless. Like children often feel. God bless them all.

Today a child's world, Johnny's world, always with promise for a joyful reunion with Papa, is about to be shattered. Only the hope of healing his father with a loving visit remains. He reaches out for the hand of his only support, Nurse Callahan. She leads him down the hall, feeling his fear as he hesitates at the threshold of the ward. She is soft in her nudging, gentle in pulling back the curtain surrounding bed number 6. Johnny jerks back, away from Nurse Callahan, and puts his hand over his mouth to muffle a scream. He has just seen a real skeleton.

A living man, but barely, with only tissue-paper-skin stretched over bones with sockets storing big brown eyes in a face sculpted to first form. Could this really be the man he expected to jump from a car, sweep him up, and swirl together on the Herriman lawn?

"Mr. Huszar, your son is here," Callahan says. The man seems to be in a trance. "Can you hear me, sir? Johnny is here. I have Johnny with me now. Here, sweetie, take hold of your father's hand. Johnny, take hold of your father's hand," she says again, stronger. She then eases the reticent child closer to the bed as his father, in punishing effort, tilts his head toward his son to acknowledge him and with further determination pushes hard to extend in very slow motion his atrophied hand. They join, and Johnny carefully sits down on the side of the bed. Ambivalent but brave, he leans over and presses his face against Papa's cheek for the touch and warmth each needs.

"As I told you," the nurse says, "your father's vocal chords are paralyzed so he won't be able to talk to you. But he can hear. And you can talk to him. We think maybe he will be able to communicate a little with his eyes," she says. "But his sight is limited, so you'll need to be up close face to face." A man in that humiliating position, unable to express himself or even move himself, yet still 'acutely aware,' has to be thinking that this is no time for guessing games. And that's what eye reading attempts would be. How could his young son read his eyes? And how could he, through the prism of aged eyes, read his son's? No, he needs desperate measures to help him talk to his son. He owes him that. Here, now, is his only chance to make it right. He is ready to reverse his angry decision of long ago, uttered in great sorrow and fear of further loss. He regrets the impulse to flee, so heavy on his heart now. He must, he has to, tell Johnny. And with every inch of his being the dying man tries. Defying nature, he forces a nanosecond guttural response by straining every blood vessel in his head and neck: and now distended, he strains again. And again. Nothing happens. Even the guttural hint is lost. It's hard to breathe around the paralysis, harder still to whisper. But that doesn't mean this father will give up: his heart is beating to keep possibility alive. It appears now that

Papa is praying. Soon he'll begin again his battle against time, armed by the best and asking very little of Him: just one moment of breath from heaven. All this with his young son nearby, exposed to the forever of these indelible unimaginable sights and sounds. Exhausted, depleted, this man with so little life left still wants to pursue. He is desperate to unveil the truth to Johnny. So again and lastly he works even harder that he might reach below the frozen barrier of his throat to a pinpoint pocket of air ready to ascend.

Miracles do happen, portioned from above as gifts of grace. And when they occur, it is in God's timing. Always. Wishes to come true are less likely to respond, but we continue to treasure fairytales and legends: their secular pleasure from pages of creative imagination and heroic storytelling rich in life lessons subtly teaching from within. Frank Huszar is not new to the experience of unanswered prayer. Didn't he plead, cry, and beg for a miracle, that his beloved Lizzie be spared the lethal blight of the 1918 flu pandemic? And didn't she die regardless of all his prayers? That she was one of many millions of people stricken by the deadly illness while so many others escaped made no sense to him, made him angry. She was so kind to others—lovely in every way, and only twenty-nine years old—that he just couldn't understand why she was taken. Finally he came to believe it was predestined: out of his hands, and she safely in God's. And that enabled him to cope better in his grief. Although the miracle he had prayed for never reached fulfillment, he could accept that losing Lizzie had true purpose, God's will for her, and that one day it would be revealed to him. That answer is near.

#

By now Frank is beyond any expectation of helpful intervention, his bodily pain abated in accordance with end of life biology, and his pending death no longer feared. What is singularly important right now is his continuing to try to talk to his son: he would be unable to accomplish any heroic efforts from a body so frail were it not for an inborn parental force and a medical phenomenon called **terminal restlessness**. In a way, TR is a kind of deathbed energy patients sometimes receive and endure. It's not a hopeful sign, rather more like wild agitation, and it can be harmful to the patient if severe. But Frank doesn't exhibit agitation, just determination. If only he could quell his need to find voice these last moments and embrace the presence and purity of his young son sitting so close. But internally, physiologically, he simply cannot relax. His body is not his anymore. Frank knows Johnny's spirit is sweet and sincere and that he loves him unconditionally, remembering their life together in the garret when a little boy took such good care of his papa. He's also very aware that Johnny is a gift, mostly unopened. He mourns the years lost, as he now sees the remnants of his decisions. He clearly missed the beauty of bonding with his son. All he can hope for—or would ask for if possible in these critical moments—is Johnny's forgiveness and an ability to reveal to him, only by miracle at this point, family information he so deserves to hear. Even promise of a reunion, the bliss of being with his dearly loved Lizzie again, is not foremost in Frank's mind. His dying wish is a spiritual favor: one moment of speech. And Johnny, wanting more than anything to hear what his father has to say, needing to know whatever it is, caring not at all that he looks so ghastly, puts his hand under Papa's head, lifting it slightly so he can place his ear directly over his father's mouth. He hears nothing. But he waits.

"Are you sleeping, Papa? Can you try again, one more time? Try to find a way to whisper to me. I will listen very close." With his ear again pressed against his father's open lips, Johnny still patiently waits with hope. Papa has been trying tirelessly, but it is simply too late. It is time to rest. In that second Johnny instinctively looks up into his father's eyes. A single tear forms and makes its way down slowly, heartbeat by heartbeat, along the side of Papa's face and down onto his neck. Johnny believes that in that teardrop are the words his father fought to share. Words he now will never know. But there are these he will: cherished words from that moment when a father and son looked into each other's eyes and spoke without sound:

"I love you, my son. I love you, Papa." It is their good-bye. Papa has closed his eyes.

#

Nurse Callahan had offered to do a double shift and has been standing just outside the curtain for some time now. She hears Johnny crying.

"I can't leave him now. Not when I just found him again. I want my papa back!"

When she reenters behind the curtain to be of comfort to the little boy, he brushes her back a step from the approach he feels is too close. And she respects his wish. But he doesn't mind that she stays there with him in the enclosed area or that she sees him crying. She's crying too. He stays on the bed, cradling his father's head in his hands, a little man alone sobbing for the older man who'd also been alone. And Johnny prays, quietly so Miss Callahan doesn't hear, a little prayer to Jesus whom he knows can make miracles. "Dear Jesus: Please restore my papa to me. Please, Jesus; just like you did for Lazarus, please do that for my father, I pray. His name is Frank Huszar. I miss him. I most always missed him. But I can wait if you are busy right now. Thank you. Love, John Huszar."

And with that, Nurse Callahan steps closer and removes Johnny from his hold on his father, checks for pulse, then with stethoscope double checks for heartbeat and pulls the sheet up over the face as Johnny watches, motionless. With the compliant child at her side, she first informs her superior and then leads him away.

"Come on, sweetheart, we'll go see if there's any cocoa down in the kitchen and find a place to talk a while."

"Thank you but no, I can't. I need to get right back. I don't want to miss the next train."

The veteran nurse can see Johnny is in shock and in no condition to leave, especially so late in the night.

"It is very late now, Johnny. There won't be a train until tomorrow, I'm sure. But we can find you a place to bunk for the night." She wishes she could take him home with her to get some quality sleep, but she still has to finish her shift. And regulations would prohibit it anyway. "Poor little fella. Such a sad little thing," she cries in a whisper that Johnny will not hear.

"Maybe I can just sleep in my father's bed. Okay, Miss Callahan?"

She recoils at such a suggestion. "How deep is the need in this child that he would ask for such a thing? It breaks my heart," she says under her breath, slowly turning her head side to side. But she is good at faking facial expressions when it benefits the patient. Today she has been wearing her 'soft and kind grandmother' cover to which Johnny responds well. She clears her throat: "No, honey, I'm afraid that would be against the rules. Tell you what, though. You and me, we'll sit in the sunroom a while. I won't be going off duty anytime soon. We'll talk some, and when you get tired you can rest on the bench. I will pile up lots of blankets to make it soft."

Johnny agrees, though he can't imagine the sun ever shining in a place like this, even in the daytime. Even in the summer with its extra sun. Nurse Callahan has found the cocoa and brings it to Johnny on a tray along with vanilla wafers. She sits down across from him to rest her feet. It has been a long day with almost double walking. "I'm very sorry about your father," she says again. "We tried."

Johnny thinks she means 'tried to make his father well again.' Ever curious, his mind already reasoning, Johnny has a question for Nurse Callahan. "If my father was paralyzed today, was he also when he first came here? He couldn't have talked to me last week either, right?"

"Right," she says. Then quickly qualifies: "I suppose it's possible he could have been able to speak a little. At least perhaps whisper."

"And, maybe," Johnny posits, "he could have scribbled some words to me, do you think, Miss Callahan? His hands weren't paralyzed."

"No, they were not. They were weak, though. But I would say that yes, he probably would have been able to put a few thoughts down on paper. Difficult maybe, but possible; I'm not a doctor so I can't say for sure. But I do know that when I first started tending him almost two weeks ago, he was stronger. It still might have been difficult, but I think he could have managed a few words to you, messy writing no doubt, but legible—at least to those of us who have learned to decipher doctors' notorious handwritings.

"I'm really sorry, Johnny." She found it so important to say it again. His questions had started her thinking.

"Thank you. Me, too," he says. He's quiet for a moment, reaching his own conclusions. Sadly, he makes a statement of regret: "I think Papa wanted to tell me how to get back home." As the night progresses, he shares with Bertha Callahan, little by little, how he'd been taken away, and how he'd waited alone, and why it was so very important for him to hear or read his father's parting message.

"But surely, dear, you will be able to find your aunts someday. There are ways," she says, wanting so much to be encouraging. "Perhaps the police could help with contact information. They keep lots of records, and also the sheriff, or any official officer, knows how to search for that kind of information."

Johnny feels so helpless in this dilemma: "I don't even know how to begin. It will be hard because you see, I don't know if they have moved away to another town or maybe another state, or if one or two got married and changed their names. My uncle didn't stay by my aunts; he was a traveling person most of the time. I don't know where are [sic] the places he goes to."

"Well, I know what you can do," Nurse Callahan says with a smile of success. "Ask your headmaster at Herriman to write a letter to the town where you used to live. They probably keep property and automobile records perhaps even birth records regarding their residents right there; and certainly, they have personal knowledge of local townsmen. I really think that they can tell you if any of your family still lives there or where they may now be located." It pleases her to think she may have solved the little boy's problem. The suggestions she offered are excellent leads. Johnny is aware of that and is appreciative.

However, his overriding obstacle impedes any research. He fidgets a bit, not wanting to disappoint this nice lady, and attempts a smile as he looks at the kind face of Nurse Callahan and confesses: "I'm sorry, but I can't do that, Miss Callahan. I wish I could, for sure. Mr. Eckard would be willing to write the letter, I think. But you see, I don't even remember the name of where I lived. Where I belong."

#

Johnny faithfully waits for the answer to his prayer for Papa getting another life, not yet forthcoming but still possible. He begins to feel the burden of arriving late, letting his father lie alone when he needed him most, at his bedside; when he was still able to talk. When it was fair. The little orphan understands those days were special and will never return. But he doesn't yet suspect the devil behind the consequences he already suffers: the first being the robbery of those days. And the deceit that made it happen. The willful withholding of critical communication, not one's own but fiduciary, leans toward criminal behavior. Johnny's been deliberately deprived, but his youth prevents full awareness of the depth and delicate timeline that suggests and questions a possible manipulated murder: days of a dying father hidden from son. Finally informed, child travels to his father but arrives too late for speaking or note writing. Papa is too weak, too fragile, too near death … and mute. Any opportunity for communication has passed. The extreme and extraordinary efforts to find voice are now silent.

#

Without the benefit of answered prayer, Johnny will just pretend to talk to his father like he most always did during those years of parental famine. He likes to imagine Papa being home, sitting right across from him on his cot. But he had hardly ever been on that cot. The total number of visits is insulting … not to forget illegal and harmful for the heart: emotionally and medically. Substantial food came only by friends' generosity and Johnny's ingenuity. Aimless days robbed education, healthy habits, fellowship, sufficient clothing and love, particularly for a child who waits long and alone. But Johnny decides to wean from the waiting. Of course he would love a happy answer from Jesus, but he realizes no answer is the answer, so he accepts that it is not his time for a miracle. That doesn't mean he can't still feel close to his papa. He knows him better than ever before and holds new memories of his love now, so he will just use words that fit, keeping near to him, talking to Papa whenever he wants on their own special wavelength in the frequency of love.

"I missed you so much, Papa. Why didn't we stay together? Mr. Abe said there were jobs all around. Where were you? Why didn't you come for me? Mrs. Zimmerman and all the people in the office on Schermerhorn Street had the address.

"I waited for you, Papa, every day in my heart. On Sunday afternoon I was outside siting on the front porch steps because it was visiting day, and I didn't want to miss you. I was sitting right there up front."

After a short period of grieving, Johnny returns to his responsibilities. The Eckards didn't force him, but his internal clock and compass did. He could feel it was time to get back to his schoolwork and beloved animal friends. He didn't understand it would also be therapeutic. Sunday is different now. The ritual remains the same—Johnny still waits on the steps—but the dream is different. Instead of his father, his aunts and uncle in his thoughts, and his motion pictures, he begins to imagine a new family.

"They are very nice people who live in their own little house and want to adopt. Want to adopt a son. They would come to Herriman and ask the Eckards if there was a little boy needing a family that they could adopt. And could they meet the little boy ... because you would want to know each other first. And then they could just pick me out to go home with them...." Lovely tableau. Wishful thinking. Catch a falling star.

Emotionally Johnny longs for this family for quite a while. Intellectually he recognizes he is close to being too old. People like to adopt babies. He needs to give up the fantasy and get off the steps, but he doesn't let go easily.

It would be another loss.

PART TWO

Chapter XIII

It is one of those significant moments in life, a plate shift, when our intended path quivers, and what we do resets the stage and reassembles the players forever.

A glance, deep breath, indelible image....

And a life becomes a mission.

Wave Crest Convalescent Home, a refuge for invalid children in Far Rockaway, New York, was atypical in its sprawling campus with two large residential homes, brown shingled and cozy, situated among the trees for shade, yet near enough to claim part of Rockaway Beach, a summer destination popular for its cotton white sand and Atlantic Ocean shoreline. The perfection of such a setting offered sun and solace to little, even infant, crippled and cardiac patients. Each summer suffering children, sponsored by Brooklyn Children's Aid Society, were transported from upstate to the facility by the sea, joining young longer-term residents for essential therapeutic treatment and unity. From water's edge and sand dunes, to grassy soil and live oaks, it is a backyard for children, landscaped by nature, designed for individual need—a tonic for the spirit of a disadvantaged child.

The Beeman House and Cheever House, unlike side street beach bungalows, look like actual homes: a deliberate intention to replace a sterile and painful environment with the sound of breaking waves or a soft breeze blowing through sheer curtains, soothing patients to sleep. Most medical equipment is out of sight but never the nurses. Their smiles and child-friendly personalities were part of the children's pleasure.

It is summer 1932 and John, with good pal Duke assisting, has just delivered an ambulance full of disabled, in some cases immobile, children to the convalescent center where little dreams of sand and sea do come true. It has been a year since the friends graduated from Spring Valley High School and saw their names removed from the roster of Herriman foster care. Duke moved down to Far Rockaway right away for a part-time position at Wave Crest, and John remains at The Farm as a member of the staff and resident of cottage number 8. With the quaint village he loves nearby, his church even closer, many friends to enjoy, and the new junior college opening this fall, it's a perfect environment for him. Duke is occasionally dispatched back to The Farm to help the heavy lifting of summer transfers. John continues to drive patients to the shore even though it's not part of his job description and never ever on the clock. It is a gesture of appreciation, his way of giving back to Herriman.

However, it's a very difficult gift to give: transporting young helpless and fragile little bodies, lifting them to a measure of escape, their eyes, many tearful, saying thank you when they cannot, is heartbreaking. Their plight is overwhelming, and a lesson in gratitude for those of us with unearned blessings. John's empathic nature is vulnerable to feeling their pain and brave endurance. They face so much and have so little. Some are bound in braces or in wheelchairs, or on crutches, with others breathing laboriously in the heat, several on their backs from paralysis, and others heavy laden in iron, all out of reach of his help. And it hurts him. This year is no different. Oh, but yes it is....

A thirst for tea and its consequent moment in time is about to profoundly reshape a future: John's future. It will be a very different year indeed. Life-altering. That plate shift.

#

"Before we leave let's go back in for something to drink; it's so darn hot today," John says. "Iced tea would hit the spot, but I'll be happy even with just a cup of water." They are standing on the front porch.

"No, I'm okay. Go ahead. I'll be in the truck." Duke walks away to the waiting vehicle.

John walks inside to the waiting destiny. She is sitting at the kitchen table when he first sees her. First reacts to her. It is immediate and it is overpowering: every inch of his body bubbles with an intensity of intoxication foreign to him until this very moment. He stands in awe of her, unable to turn away; mesmerized, not unlike a visitor in the gallery hall of the Louvre studying a smile. She's thin and dainty, lovely in a crisp white uniform that reflects the purity of her skin and contrasts vividly with the wavy auburn hair that frames her face. Her slender hands look purposely carved for playing the piano, and her patrician profile brings to mind formal silhouette portraits for which she could professionally pose. She is beautiful, and when she looks up for a brief second, the brilliance of crystalline blue eyes takes his breath away. They are the clarity of diamonds. In that split second the young woman squints as if seeking recognition, and when there is none, she quickly blinks back to her conversation. In that same nanosecond, Johnny, his eyes his camera now, captures the immediate image that forms on his retina and by optic nerve fast-travels to his brain, promising a constant memory, a reminder of a vision, a portrait for forever.

"Did you see her, Duke?" Johnny couldn't wait to ask as he opened the driver's side door. "The pretty nurse with auburn, almost red, hair? She was in the kitchen. Or maybe did you see her in the halls? Have you ever seen her now that you work at Wave Crest? Please say you know her!"

"Huh? What, who you talking about? How would I know what broad you mean? No, I have no idea. The only ones I really talk to are Ruth and Helen, both blonds. Real knockouts if you ask me. Now that Ruthie, she's one I wouldn't mind...." He notices his friend is dead serious and adds, "No; sorry, buddy, can't help you." After taking Duke home to his apartment and maneuvering around beach foot traffic, John speeds away from the flame of internal combustion, replaying the moment when his heart skipped a beat, or two, and everything changed but looks the same. *"I suppose I'm being foolish to indulge in such a silly fantasy. I have to pull myself together and think about what I need to do tomorrow. I don't even know her name!"*

Yet something is undeniably different. Always calm and level headed, John is surprised by feeling so anxious—like never before about anything in his entire life. He will try to forget her for now and focus on all he intends to accomplish this summer and beyond. Yet he knows at his core he will not stop thinking about the girl in the kitchen until next transfer south, with its legitimate reason for his being there, looking around for her, even inquiring about her. He can hardly wait.

The fluttering in his heart returns whenever he thinks about her, feels the power of her, envisions a first moment with her. And with that reality he feels obliged to stop seeing Dorothy Wenzel without delay. It would be unfair to her to continue, and he will tell her so. Because what he might have accepted as a comfortable compatible life with her can no longer be considered. His intellect tells him there is more. His heart confirms. So with the honesty that rules his world, John ends their long courtship and breaks a heart.

"Can't we still see each other, please, Johnny?" Dorothy asks, but he is adamant:

"No, I'm sorry, we cannot."

"My parents love you; I love you; oh, please don't stop coming around," she begs. Her sobs are piercing but not manipulating. She's just totally distraught, and John's sensitive response is to comfort her with an embrace, but he quickly realizes that it could be misleading. There may also be a second reason for his restraint: a subconscious fidelity to the girl with no name.

The separation will be painful for John, a true loss; and especially difficult to refrain from visits in the loving home where he has felt so welcome. He is very fond of Mr. and Mrs. Wenzel as they were of him. Dinners in their vaulted-ceiling satin-draped dining room had been so elegant—in deep regal red. Both are educators and John drew from them, observed their way of life, even made notes of some of their family traditions. He'd been encouraged by their belief in him and challenged by lively debates. And he will miss the friendship. But to continue to accept the gracious open arms to their home and heart would be unfair. There is no alternative. He has to do the right thing.

Work and his projects, always methodically approached, will help fill the void. He's already signed up for the new Rockland Junior College that will commence in September, eager and excited to follow a life of the mind. This energy of purpose adds hours to those required by his job as head mechanic at the Fuel & Body Shop. He tries to balance it all by regular attendance to church and a kind of therapeutic relaxation he receives when huddled over his beloved roadster coming to fruition in a boarding house backyard. When he was young and still in school, he built himself a men's 26- or maybe 28-inch bike: loving the open air on his face he pedals around the countryside and newborn towns, stopping often for an egg cream or sarsaparilla at Valley Pharmacy, a favorite place to sit with friends. So no one was surprised when Johnny decided to build a car. He will search daily for parts as he did, successfully, when he constructed his bike. He knows that with patience and a keen eye almost every essential component required for the intricate mechanical system will be found in the local treasure trove of trash. The engineering design, the esthetics, everything, will one day come together perfectly under the devoted and loving touch of a man with a dream.

He will drive his cherished black roadster, with its camel-colored fabric roof, down to Wave Crest; it will purr in precision and a high shine, and he will beam with pride when the beautiful young maiden accepts his invitation to go for a spin. He will place his hand under her elbow and help her onto the running board, and when she has adjusted her frock, he will offer his arm for balance while she moves into the brown leather seat.

He'll double check the door, go around to his own, hop in, and whisk her away. For now, though, he's riding a bike.

It was in 1931 that Johnny, new high school graduate, began a life of his own, gaining a better sense of his worth along the way. He'd been popular in school as a top student and a good catch. Unaware of the magnet within and unimpressed by his academic honors, John finds real reward in the accolades from friends. But the happiest moment of graduation week came not at the ceremony and not at the parties, but in the office of Mr. Eckard in the after-dinner hours, a lambent moon already positioned for the occasion, a brandied coffee prepared by Margaret to kindle the mood. It was then that they handed John the official letter. To his surprise, it was from Edward W. Macy, general director of the Brooklyn Children's Aid Society, and former World War I decorated major who'd taught John so much from edifying conversations whenever he came up to audit Herriman. History, literature, a splash of math, and personal accounts of the war were on the menu, and Johnny always looked forward to a next visit. The cerebral relationship enriched both: for the child more knowledge, for the widower insight into a younger generation. It was to be an everlasting bond.

By formal letter Mr. Macy was citing John's contributions to Herriman, thanking him on behalf of the organization and himself; inviting him to stay on as an employee of the system, assigned to The Farm in any role he and the Eckards choose if, of course, it meets his needs.

#

A short lull after the stock market crash belied the Depression ahead. But in late summer 1930 there had been joblessness and economic trauma, predicting poverty and exponential ruin. The evidence of financial harm increased in 1931, a prelude to the two years following—1932 and 1933— that suffered most heavily from hunger, unemployment, loss of shelter, and saddest, loss of dignity. The fiscal assault and its ashes of devastation became known as the Great Depression, during which the need for utter basics was ravenous. It was mid 1931 when John saw prophetic signs of famine for the country and the value of a role at Herriman. Opportunities for adequate work all around over the country were diminishing. He will accept Mr. Macy's offer, but it is not from financial fear: it is because he feels he has a debt to pay. With all that Herriman has provided him, how could he not give back? Could he really walk away from the burdens of a busy farm business when it's obvious they are in serious trouble? His postgraduation plan to continue as a volunteer ambulance driver does not need to end, and the goal to satisfy a self-proclaimed debt to his alma mater will not be affected. This, then, is John's opportunity 'to do good.' Yes, he must take it.

#

Accompanying the letter from his mentor was a gift, a beautifully leather-bound collection of Shakespeare's Sonnets—a revered classic introduced to John by Mr. Macy several years earlier. Then it was the Eckards' turn, and they presented him with still another treasure, frayed at the edges, spine broken from overuse, but equally beautiful in sentiment: Robert Louis Stevenson's *Treasure Island*, John's favorite so many years ago when he first discovered the school library and began to devour its riches. Graduating to other authors, he still returned loyally to his literary friend—and there was little doubt the book had been in his hands almost as often as on the shelf. It had simply become his book, and Margaret wanted him to have it. Not a new one. She wanted him to have the very copy that had been his treasure in the early days. As he had been hers. Definitely a memorable evening ... John was overwhelmed by unexpected gifts and affection. It had also been a revealing evening: the Eckards were uncharacteristically open with their feelings. They spoke directly from the heart: fidgeting, not knowing how far to go, how disloyal they dared be. The quasi-parents played dangerously.

"Johnny, John now, your school record has been superb, both here and over at Spring Valley High. And in your other work as well: your chores, willingness to cooperate and participate, even initiate, and readiness to share, went well beyond expectation," Margaret says. "You've been a bright light up here, a spark plug igniting the others, actually turning some of the borderline boys around. We want you to know you will always be an indelible part of our lives." Her voice began to break, and her husband deftly intervened.

"What she's really trying to get to, John, is that we wish we could help you more in your educational pursuits. You've got such a good mind and so much talent to go with it: if we could, we'd invest in that talent.

"But we can only afford to educate one. And, of course, it must be our son. Our duty is to Stephen. But if truth be known, you are the one we should be sending off to the Ivy League school in September. We are so sorry, heart sorry, that we cannot make it possible for you."

"Oh, no sir, you've helped me so much already; I couldn't accept any more assistance even if you were in a financial position to offer, so please don't give it another thought. It would never have entered my mind if you hadn't brought it up, so let's forget it. You've been a good guardian. That's what I will remember.

"And don't worry about me. I'll read and I'll study, and I'll never stop learning. It's a love of education that began when I was young and given the gift of a very big book. You've probably seen it upstairs on my shelf, the *World History Book*, well worn and without updates but still a dependable and enriching friend for me."

"Yes, I've noticed that book up there: impressive," Baynard says. "Now, would you allow us to extend a little helping hand to you, John?"

He's like a child eager to tell a secret, and his eyes dance with his own happiness.

"Mrs. Eckard and I would like to invite you to stay on here, living at Herriman, if indeed you intend to accept Mr. Macy's offer. It will save you the expense of room and board at Miss Bessie's place. Unless, of course, you feel an urgency to be completely independent, which we would understand."

Not surprising, it had been Margaret's idea, selfish in part, her way of having John around a while longer; of delaying the day he would move out of her life completely. Her husband had agreed right away. He may have sensed her motivation, but she is harmless now. The injustice of the past had been pardoned years ago. Someday the options will run out for Margaret. They would have long ago if Johnny had held her accountable; he could have asked Mr. Macy for a transfer downstate to one of their Long Island boarding homes. Instead, he forgave, and that allowed him to move on in a spirit of love and harmony within the Eckard family. Margaret understood there would be competing options for John, but for the present time she is pleased with her solution. John's answer, if in the affirmative, would be an asset for all of Herriman.

"With your being on staff, it would be quite acceptable and legitimate from a budgetary perspective to offer you continued residency here," Baynard says, lighting his pipe. "Now we realize a man needs his privacy: it wouldn't do for you to remain upstairs in a single room so close to others. There would be no problem converting one of the small buildings out back, probably number 8, into a little apartment for you. Heck, you could do it all yourself. You're the carpenter around here. Suit it to your taste. Resurrect and upholster some of the old pieces of furniture stored up in the attic. Perhaps build inside shutters to cover the windows: you can do it all and well. Just look at what you've accomplished here in this house, inside and out, under the guise of fun, a hobby."

"Shut up!" Margaret wants to scream. She's edgy from Baynard's rambling, afraid he will talk Johnny right out the door. "He better not of [sic] spoiled a good plan with that stupid independence comment!" Of course, her words are only in silent sentences.

"By the way, John, I hear you'll be building a car for yourself," Baynard says. "And that you're gonna [sic] bring it to life in the old deserted garage out back of Miss Bessie's place."

John laughs: "Well, I plan to. But it's an enormous attempt. I just hope one of these years I will have a road-worthy vehicle of my own."

"You will," the Eckards say in unison. "And, of course, there's room enough in one of the garages here for you to build your car in all kinds of weather if you like," Baynard adds for good will.

"Thank you for being so kind, Mr. Eckard. And I do accept your invite to live here. Wow, so much is being offered to me—I'm at a loss for words. Salary from the Schermerhorn office, living quarters here—and because I know you both so well, I know you're talking meals too—but it's just too generous. The whole package is over the top. So no discussion: I pay full rent and an additional meal tab every month, or if you prefer biweekly. And let's clarify my responsibilities in the new position that Mr. Macy seems to have created: I want to be sure I earn all that I receive." He looks at them quizzically, awaiting confirmation.

"Just keep on being Mr. Fix-It," Baynard says. "That way I manage to avoid the struggle of handyman like I've been doing almost ever since you arrived, bringing your natural talent with you. Thank goodness. It was such a blessing. And I learned.... But I confess I still hide behind the experts for the important stuff. That's my method of accomplishment.

"Seriously, though, you'll oversee planting and harvest, help with the cows: by that I mean milking when in a pinch—no pun intended," he chuckles, "and any animals needing special attention. You'll make repairs at the house and peripheral buildings, including barn: essentially build up all that's about to fall down.

"I'd like you to serve as supervisor of the property grounds and part-time employees, as well as alternating weekends 'on call' for emergencies."

All three giggle, remembering the crisis of the Windsor chair: demolition, unintended, from their heavyweight housekeeper and occasional cook, Fiona. She was walking evidence of her culinary interests.

"In keeping with a professional relationship," Baynard says, "you will be on a day shift, your hours recorded for your benefit, but never counted if related to school attendance or collateral, like library or field trips when the junior college opens. We believe in education and promote it at every turn."

Placing his coffee cup on the butler's tray table, John rises from his seat. He walks over to Mr. Eckard and shakes his hand. "Thanks again, sir.

It'll be great to hang around longer here at Herriman, my home." That was enough, that and their handshake, a little stronger than usual.

With the battered book clasped tightly in his left hand, John then walks to Mrs. Eckard. This time it is he who kneels down, eye to eye, while she remains seated, regal in a Queen Anne chair covered in burgundy and gold threaded brocade. "Thank you for this." He shakes his head slightly as if disbelieving the wonder of it all. "It is a treasure that will stay with me always." He would have said more but the lump in his throat and tears about to fall are too much to fight against.

He goes upstairs. Baynard helps Margaret from her chair and they walk to the door, standing there a moment, gazing back at the semicircle of empty chairs. It has the feel of a theater after the final curtain fell.

Alone now, John reflects on this memorable graduation week, its unexpected warm wishes and thoughtful, irreplaceable gifts. He is pleased with the presents, awards, and friendships, but understands their much deeper significance: they are first fruits, evidence of his resolve when as a young boy returning from the dark days of his father's death he intuitively knew to press on, avoid judgment, put the questions aside, and count his blessings. There were many: he wasn't hungry, wasn't a walking target on uncertain streets, slept in a real bed with no rats, and had a place to call home. He's so thankful for that home today: a post-Coney Island childhood, happy school years, a farm life, even subtle parenting. He wonders where he would be if he had allowed grief and blame to set his path. Best of all, beyond the tangible, Johnny lived in confidence, the kind that comes with love and belonging—feeling his place in the Eckard family was genuine. And he was gratefully aware of how well the children accepted his presence in their lives without jealousy of any kind. He felt safe with the family, albeit in truth an institutional relationship. Never would he risk losing the connection. They were all he had, and he valued his inclusion.

Nevertheless he had suspicions, carried quietly through the years. They would never be revealed, of course, nor would he ever regret his tough-to-deliver forgiveness. He forgave an unbelievable offense because we're taught to and it's freeing, but it also met his need to be at peace and not haunted by an act without reason. As much as he tried, however, Johnny couldn't quite forget Nurse Callahan and what she had said about Papa possibly whispering to him a week or two earlier, or at least able to scribble a note one week earlier than his arrival allowed. Nor could he forget her words, "We tried." At first, he thought she meant medical efforts to help his father survive. And he hoped that to be true. So much so that if an alternative theory entered his mind by way of a cold chill, he immediately rejected it. He didn't want to believe those words could mean that the hospital had tried hard to bring him to his father in time. But a heart holds truth, and Johnny, wishing against instinct, reluctantly suspects that Mrs. Eckard initiated the withholding of the first telegram. His understanding of Baynard, having spent substantial hours with him, does not allow for deceit. He is a gentleman: respectful, conciliatory, kind. He honors his wife but also holds to his values. Perhaps in listening to her persuasive rhetoric he tries too hard to see her side, and with little debate, agrees too soon to a truce. So John feels the gentle man cannot fully be blamed: it was manipulation that caused him to defer to his wife, and without his reading the impassioned first telegram, allowed its message to marinate in the possession of evil. Under the art of influence, Baynard dishonored the need of a dying father and therefore became complicit in a morally wrong crime. Along with his wife Margaret, they secreted the message that made the difference between John's father being able to speak to his son and the paralysis of voice that prevented him from sharing what he so needed to say to his boy.

It was the second message that forced Baynard to reveal to Johnny his father's urgent condition and permit him to travel to his bedside. Not surprising, when the child arrives it is too late for words: his father can no longer speak. The damage is done, not by death, but by days hidden, along with vital family information concealed. Days and words that had belonged to Johnny. To be so cavalier with irreplaceable moments in the lives of others is inexcusable, and yet she, they, were excused: forgiven by the very person so deeply harmed. Now here tonight, boyhood behind, a lovely evening just ended, John is both peaceful and inspired by the events of the celebratory graduation week, now at low ebb. It was a time of encouragement by people he never expected to care, and their kind words energized him. Yet there's something odd about this new spirit of abundance in the air: yes, pomp and circumstance can do that. But John is not susceptible to praise and adulation. No, it's not like that. The only time anyone will ever see shoulders-back pride in the man is when he completes his project and introduces his precious new home-built car around town. What he's feeling he just can't figure out: maybe anxiety about the ambitious hobby ahead. No, he loves to create and it has a calming effect on him. This feeling can't be linked to the car, or better said, 'someday car.' And it's not emotional; not a conscious thought; not a sensation; not foreboding; nor euphoric… it's, "Oh yes, right, it's cautionary."

Of course, he remembers now. He knows exactly what it is: unfinished business. Graduation from high school usually coincides with release from the auspices of the Brooklyn Children's Aid Society at age eighteen. And John has just turned eighteen. The fiduciary relationship has ended: he is no longer a ward of the state, that awful sounding definition of an abandoned child in foster care. He is free from the system except for one very important detail: the return of a little coin changer, his beloved piece of property taken away almost by force, but in the end by policy and a hard-fought promise for "safe storage and return to owner at discharge."

In typical Johnny self-talk, he muses, "*I should probably go down to the Schermerhorn office tomorrow before I start the new job. The Eckards won't mind. In fact, I think there's some kind of exit interview that has to happen, so I can take care of that too. I just hope there's no problem reclaiming my property: I won't leave without the coin changer and its rightful contents.*"

John's tired now after such a busy bountiful day and evening. He should sleep well in the afterglow of so many predictions of triumph for his future.

#

Even after ten years, not much is different at the headquarters of the Brooklyn Children's Aid Society. The austere waiting area still offers old hardwood chairs, though there is a section for children now with smaller chairs and lots of pillows, and colorful books to ease the long wait for the hoped-for happy ending down the hall. John takes a seat, this time with a number.

"May I help you?" a young woman asks.

And John recites his story, for which she has no understanding.

"I will have to get someone up here to talk to you. I've never heard about any special room around here. But who am I? Only a front desk typist who also runs errands."

"Well, that's important work," John says for encouragement. "How about Mrs. Rupley? Is she still here? She knows everything about the coin changer. I should go down to her office; she might be here and just too far on the other side of the building for you to know."

"Could be. I just never heard of her. Hey, Carmella, come mere [sic] a sec," she calls, waving her over. "You been [sic] working here a long time, so do you know a Mrs. Rupley?"

"Nope, and I'm going on lunch break right now, sorry I can't help."

Mary, the receptionist's name as John now knows, says he shouldn't go down the hall, but that she will call somebody. A supervisor and another person with a title arrive and agree to search lost and found for the item. That troubles John: it's not the correct category. His property was well documented Mrs. Rupley had said, and he wants to find someone who knows her and can contact her if the men return empty handed. They do. And they apologize for the unsuccessful search offering to compensate him the cost of a coin changer plus the 85 cents.

John attempts to explain the emotional value of his father's gift, and the care with which Mrs. Rupley identified and placed into safekeeping the little coin changer with its 85 cents inside. It doesn't make an impression on the two midlevel uninspired workers, however. But Johnny, true to his intent, will not go easily into acceptance. He still wants to talk to these men. Someone has to know something. So he follows them down the hall and enters the first office right behind man number 1; and, absent any gesture of welcome, sits himself down in a chair directly facing the man now at his desk. He's startled by this visitor and fiddles with a pen for a moment, deciding to cough and clear his throat for some kind of power, and points to the door ordering in his deepest voice, "I want you to leave my office now." But John ignores the man's discomfort.

"My name is John Huszar, and I don't intend to take much of your time, sir, but I do think there's some way to find the missing item with its adjunct coins that were entrusted to the Brooklyn Children's Aid Society. I need to explore every avenue: the first is how to locate the once employed Mrs. Rupley. I mentioned her out there at the reception area, but couldn't get any information to when I asked if anyone knew her. That's why I'm sitting here. Do you know her?"

"Can't say that I do," he says, looking away toward the window. "I don't remember that name. Or maybe I do a little. I'm just not sure."

"Okay Mr. um … I'm sorry, what is your name? Thank you, Mr. Dewy Parker, nice to meet you," John says, leaning over the desk to extend his hand. Not surprisingly, the man does not reciprocate. So John just simply sits back and continues to question. "Do you happen to have a list of employees or a local telephone book?"

"No, but I think I can get one. James, my buddy next door … oh, here he is.…"

"Come on, Dew," James interrupts, "hurry, we gotta [sic] go. The boss says everybody has to be looking for some 'gold plated with diamonds' coin changer. So come on, get moving." On second thought, James pauses to clarify with Dewy: "You know I'm kidding about the diamond remark, right?" he asks to rid any possible confusion, unaware of John's presence.

He's horrified once he sees him, and begins to apologize, but Johnny minimizes the mockery. "No, no: don't bother about an apology," he says as he stands up. "I wish it were true: I would be a rich man. I do expect to find it, but without the dazzle." Left behind, Johnny goes out into the hall of chaos. Apparently the boss, just mentioned by James, has enlisted his troop for duty of a different kind. And while this turn of event is deeply appreciated by John, it is also curious: "*All of a sudden so much interest in just one man's personal problem? I wonder … why all the noise?*" *John says aloud* but James is already out of sight. Johnny does want the help, but not to the exclusion of all else. He's feeling very guilty.

"One cheap little item you can buy in any 'five and dime' goes missing and gets all this attention," the designated hunters are saying among themselves. And one man remarks, "This is far more interesting than the real serious stuff ever gets!" Another says, "Never seen this kinda [sic] big time target mission around here. Not ever!" Johnny is speechless, in awe of, but also ashamed of, such mobilization. It is, of course, extremely important to him to find his own coin changer, but maybe not by an all-out effort organized so quickly by behind-the-scene voices. It makes him think perhaps Mr. Macy could be involved….

Calvin, man of creative lunches for a whole city block of employees, scours his kitchen utensils to make sure the coin changer wasn't mistaken for a cooking gadget; Jimmy, the maintenance man, is searching every nook and cranny in the basement that holds his tools and tests his talents; longtime favorite janitor, CJ, is checking all the familiar hiding places— coal bin included—that devious people use before they're found and fired; and Charles, the building manager in charge, has been peeking into hall closets and empty offices with high shelves, and desks with drawers or rooms with piles of cardboard boxes, most of them closed and bound with tape, awaiting a ride to the warehouse. Conference rooms are not very secure, but he checks in there anyway.

A short while later he comes back and begins walking the hall again, head turning, looking all around as he had done earlier. But this time he's looking for Johnny. He finds him, and with a wide smile of thanksgiving only a man with his job on the line would wear, hands John his coin changer. He has even counted the coins to confirm a perfect return. And yes, of course, John will count too, but privately. He expects nothing further in regard to the issue, and therefore avoids dispute.

Although my father did say to me, decades later when sharing the experience, that he was quite certain the coins returned that day were not the initial three quarters and two nickels: they were too shiny. With sharp eighteen-year-old vivid picture memory he had immediately known and would remember the contours of his coins, and the touch, that feel of built-in dirt and grease in tiny grooves that add shadow and a kind of grey metal color to them. Indeed, he could distinguish the difference between well worn and newly minted.

But it wasn't a little boy's issue anymore. By prayer and unrelenting intention, along with extraordinary help, the celebrity coin changer was again in Johnny's possession. His loss was restored. A gift came home.

Now summer 1933, and the molasses moving months of waiting are finally over for John. He no longer has to picture the Wave Crest houses cooled by balmy winds of the Atlantic, sheltered by sweeping sand dunes, and shaded by live oak trees that guard his love. Nor does he need to visualize her in the kitchen, sitting at the table, her hair blowing gently from the breeze that filters through an open window. Because he will be there: and he will find her.

John drove alone that fragrant day in early June. At his arrival, a male orderly came out to assist. They removed the children from the ambulance and delivered them to their area after which the aid returned to his usual duties. John secures his little patients in their cribs and cubicles, followed closely by the nurses who would clean and comfort and soon feed them.

He says good-bye to each one in whatever way possible, answers questions for the attendants, and smiles his way out to the hall. He completes his paperwork at a vacant desk, stands up, freshens up, and takes a deep breath for composure. He is ready to meet her and knows just where to go. But the kitchen is empty, off script. Everyone is engrossed in their work made more burdensome by the new arrivals. There is little conversation, except that which pertains to the children. Yet John sees no barrier: she will undoubtedly be in one of the wards tending to the helpless. So he walks the corridors, peeks into the dorm and a room or two, but there is no way to gently interrupt. Children are being cared for. He will not intrude. And with no sight of her anywhere, not even Duke around, he might as well go home.

But first he returns to the kitchen—still unpopulated—and accepts refreshments from a large tray with a note, "Help yourself." Crackers and hard cheese, fruits that don't easily wilt, carrots and company, and the main attraction—brownies and chocolate chip cookies—are minimally represented on John's paper plate. He eats quickly so as to be unencumbered for the second walk around the halls that he has just decided to take. He wants to include Cheever House this time. Unsuccessful at every turn, John heads back to the ambulance truck. The children have been safely delivered. He has done his job. It's time to go. A verbal pep talk becomes a companion for the long ride home: "All right, so not this trip. Next time. And there will be a next time." When he tires of the repetition, he can always sing. Well, not always, but that night. You see, there are only two venues available for John's type of musical talent: the shower and a moving car at high speed. And as he has been saying over and over to himself, "There will be a next time," there was: the very next summer.

Two years from first glance. John's interest in the mystery girl is still alive, undiminished, untouched by time, and his heartbeat on high alert as he approaches once again the threshold of hope. The posture of promise and smile of proximity, the bounce in his steps that speak joy, are blighted once again. He has attempted conversations, walked the halls in each house, even asked a nurse who seemed confused about the day's schedule.

"I don't know anybody like you ask. I am new here on staff. Sorry, but I have to go now," she said.

And John just stands there, defeated and depleted, as he watches the young woman hurry down the hall. Had he ventured over to the ocean that day he would have found her. She lay just on the other side of the dunes, sunbathing alone before starting the four to midnight shift she'd switched to help her best friend, Alva. A mound of sand was all that separated them. That, and another year.

\#

John leaves a note. *Hey, Duke, sorry I missed you this trip. Want to ask you something—hope you'll drop me a line and let me know. Couple years ago there was a nurse working at WC and I asked you about her. You didn't know her then. She has auburn hair, bue eyes, very pretty, and I first saw her in the kitchen. At least I think I did, but I'm beginning to wonder if it's just a dream. Do you know whom I mean? Is there such a person? Do you know her by now? Or at least have you seen her? If you do know her, could you wrangle an introduction? Please reply. Regards, John*

Duke was a simple man and not really a caring kind of guy, so receiving that letter meant nothing to him. Except his pride. "Never mind about her, snippy little thing turning me down like that," he says in resurrected anger. "She deserves to be ignored. I'm not writing no [sic] letter back. No way. No more about her! She don't [sic] exist!" Thankfully he's talking privately to himself. "Plus Johnny deserves better than a high and mighty dame anyway." What he really means of course, is he, 'The Duke,' did not deserve her rejection.

On second thought, he decides to respond.

John, good to hear from you. Catch you next time. No, don't know of anyone here fitting that description. Maybe she already quit. There's a big turnover of girls here. They look for husbands, and when they find somebody they up and quit to have babies. Sorry, pal, she's probably pushing one of them [sic] prams around by now. Ain't you and Dorothy getting along? Don't let a good one get away. Later, Duke.

The words rolled over John like a wet sand-filled beach ball. His hoped-for romance lost its luster. Anticipation for the transfer of 1935, if even there would be one, slowed into sadness. The system was changing. Congress, after passing its first federal program of assistance in 1933, the Federal Emergency Relief Fund, was busy enacting a broader package to be established as the Social Security Service. A ripple effect from budget cuts could possibly affect the Brooklyn Children's Aid Society—but God is good, and John is soon back again on the annual assignment to Wave Crest. His heart breaks all over again when he sees repeat children, as most of them are, and lifts a frail, sometimes immovable, body from "chains that bind" in so many ways. Orthopedic intervention, medical devices, and lifesaving equipment assist but rarely cure. The children know that, and they ask for very little. Their battles may be different but the destination is always the same: comfort. That he can provide, though regretfully not from resources of his own yet, a climate of happy change—a way to be close to the sand, touch a toe to an aging wave, or feel the frothy foam just whipped up by waves in their journey to shore; or simply rest, not so close to the edge but back a bit, and breathe in the healing sea air lightly seasoned by salt—is deeply rewarding. If only the girl with no name were still unmarried, still on staff, and waiting for him at the back entrance double-door, his trip would be complete. Yes, the desire to know her lingers even though John has worked hard all year to put her out of his mind. She belongs to someone else: might even be a mother now. And yet his full-time job, work on the car, studies, and church commitments are not enough to soothe the wound of missed opportunity.

CHAPTER XIV

Crowell Hadden is integral to Wave Crest, wearing many hats and tending many bruises. Almost always on duty as senior nurse, teacher, and housemother to the staff of young nurses, most living in the dormitory, her presence promises resolution. She is a dear lady whose gruff exterior barely hides the love and interest in others that is her life. John found her pleasant when once they worked together unloading the children and when passing in the hall, but each time she was too busy to approach. Today, however, she invites him to "sit a spell" before making his long drive upstate, and it is her warmth, a sort of soothing grandmother, counselor, confidant, to which he responds. They are at the kitchen table—same one; where is she?—but John is not drinking his coffee, only tracing around the edges of the cup, repeatedly. He considers it for a moment, then allows her kind nature to embolden him enough to ask the question he hopes will not be out of line. It is not. In fact, it is well received.

"Oh, you must mean Mabel Castle," she answers. Her smile is broad and her wink a bit flirty. "Can't be anyone else fitting that description but my Mabel." If one is to find a flaw in Crowell it is favoritism, sometimes lacking concealment. So she does exist....

"But why, John, do you say 'used to' work here? She still does."

In a mixture of unexpected elation and desire to punch a friend, John's heart is racing. But before he can even speak, he hears the news of poor timing. "Unfortunately, she's not on duty today. Mabel worked a lot of overtime and long weekend shifts recently, so I sent her home for this approaching weekend; especially since a sister is getting married, and there's a bridal shower I want her to be able to attend." Crowell does not miss the disappointment in his eyes. "I'm so sorry," she says.

"No, no, that's fine. Perhaps next time… I've really got to be going soon, anyway. But maybe when I'm here again I, well, I would like to meet her." There it is, out and done: bold and honest.

"Of course, John, yes: we'll work it out somehow," she says as they shake hands good-bye.

#

"Forthright. Sincere. I like that. Hope he does get to meet her," Crowell says aloud to the now empty kitchen as she washes their cups. This time John drives home experiencing joy he's never known. She is real: she has a name! At last there is something to hold onto. The next step will be the introduction! The odyssey is far from over. Johnny asks to drive the end-of-summer trip, but other plans are already etched in granite and he is denied. Throughout the year he's tempted to alter his schedule and make a personal visit to Wave Crest—enjoy a weekend away: stay with his friend… but he has no friend there now: Duke has shown him that. No, he will wait. Let it happen in God's time. And when the next summer arrives, John is ready for Wave Crest, convinced he will finally be meeting Mabel.

With knowing her name he feels close to her, and Crowell wants to introduce them, so in the few short hours allotted him he will begin the process of undoing any suitor's plan, simply by way of easing into conversation after Crowell's job is done. Translated that means winning Mabel over with genuine interest and an open heart. And a smile he can't help.

"Oh, I'm so sorry, John," Crowell says. "Mabel isn't here this time either. In fact, she's in the hospital. Don't worry," she says, putting up her hands to stop his thoughts, "she will be fine." A persistent young man, she recalls. Disappointed once again. "Tell you what, though. The hospital, St. Joseph, is right nearby: you've seen it for sure, 327 Beach 19th Street. I bet if you hurry you can make it before visiting hours are over." Crowell is shocked that she blurted that out. Ah, but she is glad she did. He'd been too polite to ask more questions, and there was just something about the urgency of the young man that appealed to her romantic side, not often revealed. She sees elegance in him. He is different from the guys on staff—though they're good people—and most of those typical outsiders who come to court the girls. He is a real man. Urbane and oh so handsome, but down to earth and very kind, she can tell. And just because he isn't the swaggering or aggressive type doesn't mean he isn't strong and capable. He has it all: a total man, just like James had been, may his soul rest in peace. She always thought they broke the mold after the perfection of her dear husband. Not so, it seems. She isn't absolutely sure Mabel measures up, however: always bell of the ball and prone to constant attention. But Crowell already trusts John's acumen. He will be an intelligent judge.

"Oh, thank you so much, Crowell. I'm on my way," John says almost in song.

#

"Let me see," says the young woman at the hospital's welcome desk. John's hands are clammy, his throat dry. "Castle … um, oh here it is. She's in room 306"—and John rushes to the hall as the girl shouts—"Oh no, please wait a minute, sir; don't go yet." He turns to hear her say in a lower voice, "It's noted over here that she has been discharged. Yes, I see where she was discharged this morning. Sorry."

The receptionist all of a sudden feels guilty for having checked the records, having done her job. She sees how that disappointment has defeated the man standing before her. Just moments ago the handsome—yes, she had noticed—man's face was glowing with victory. Now it projects failure. His eyes appear unfocused for a second as he blinks furiously to adjust from the shock. And when he turns and walks away, so destroyed, his emptiness so acute, the young girl is left with the weight of his sadness.

He returns to Wave Crest in full control, hoping to see Crowell and thank her again for the suggestion of the hospital visit. When he finds her on a five-minute break standing in the hall poised to enter the next private therapy room, he has just enough time to tell of the turn of event, brushing off the incident with a light laugh. So when he leaves, Crowell brushes it aside too, and never even mentions it to Mabel. Why would she? An unsuccessful visit from a stranger would require too much explanation.

#

A next attempt, heading south, this time with an assistant assigned temporarily to The Farm, John is forced out of his musings by the younger man.

"Hey, John, what's with you? I've been telling you to slow down and you pay no attention. We're gonna [sic] wreck! Where do you think you're going, to a fire or something?"

John doesn't look his way but smiles to himself and says, "Yes, sort of. But you're right. I'll cool it." A while later, Jess Banneman opens up the dialogue again. He is sincerely concerned. "What is it with you, John? You seem so preoccupied, so intense. Is anything wrong?"

"No. Really. I'm fine."

"Maybe his friends in Spring Valley and Herriman, even Duke at Wave Crest, are right," Jess begins to think. He's heard the comments, not gossip, but honest worry that travels the Children's Aid Society grapevine. They're thinking John's turning into a recluse, pining away, or worse: they're afraid he could be ill, that the way he overextends himself physically with work, his 'personal car building,' Sunday school, Wednesday night church, and transportation duties are taking a toll. That he's suffering alone, keeping those who care about him at a distance.

If John had been aware of their fears, he would have been amused and found their interest in him endearing, quickly and easily assuaging all doubts. But it never occurred to him that he was causing concern and so much attention. He is simply leading a disciplined, celibate life because he is a man of commitment, hard work, and a strong code of ethics that began as a child on his own, alone in Coney Island. The culture there is binary: either the dark of debauchery or the light of goodness. The little boy had chosen the latter, a source to which he still adheres.

"Talk to me, John; something's not right," Jess says.

"But Jess, I'm telling you nothing's wrong. Really. I'm just in a hurry to get down to Wave Crest this time. There's a girl I want to meet."

"Okay, so you risk never seeing her at all? That makes sense," Jess says with sarcasm not lost. "Try to think 'Arrive alive,'" he continues, "so that you can actually reach your destination."

"Understood," John says. Jess soon realizes that even though well intended he'd been insubordinate to John, senior by several months and man in charge of today's transfers.

"I apologize, John: I've been out of line."

"Thank you. I accept your apology." Jess now feels a need to ingratiate himself back into John's favor: "She must be very special. You seem totally engrossed in thinking of just of the idea of her, Johnny. What's her name?"

"Mabel." Just saying it is exciting for him.

"You don't mean Mabel Castle, do you?" Jess asks with renewed interest.

"Well, as a matter of fact, I do. She works at Wave Crest. You must know her down there.

"Yes, kinda: I work in the office, and my little brother was a day patient there for special physical exercises." He's getting closer.

"Thank you, God," John says quietly. He means for sending Jess as a possible channel to Mabel, but he's mindful of acknowledging the brother, too: "Is he doing okay now, your brother? They do remarkable work with the children," John says.

"Yeah, he's good. He can never play sports, but he can walk. That's the miracle," Jess says.

"Yes, a miracle," John agrees, elevating Jess to angelic purpose. For Jess it's no big deal knowing Mabel. For John it's a major breakthrough, a way through. "Tell me about her, Jess. Do you know Mabel well?"

"Nobody knows Mabel Castle well. Oh, she's real sweet to the children: they adore her. But to us guys, well she was always sort of unreachable. Off limits. All three are that way. The Castle Girls: watch out for them!

"Her two sisters, both good-looking too, would come down once in a while to go on the beach. But they always set themselves apart—like they are better than the rest of us. Best advice I can give you, John, is to just forget about it. She's real popular with the guys. Rich ones. Those that are 'going places,' as they say.

"Her father was big in real estate a while back; bought land and built nice little houses out on the island, several in Oceanside I know. She told me she liked to go out there to Oceanside and visit with her English grandmother for afternoon tea. The lady lived in one of the houses her son, Alfred, Mabel's father, built on a street he named for her, Castleton Court. I remember because it sounds so British.

"Young Mary Jane Davidson and Robert Castle had emigrated from London after being told they could not marry. Her father held a prestigious role in the Queens Foot Guards at Buckingham Palace, camera ready in full dress red tunic and bearskin hat, where he served Her Majesty with honor—and caste," [sic: play on word] "his daughter away in anger," Jess says.

It is a story fit for a granddaughter to relish. And Mabel is happily animated in sharing her family's history. Plus Jess is a good listener. Makes one wonder if judging others as 'beneath' and therefore 'unacceptable' brought the father long-lasting satisfaction or a future marred with painful loss, and shame. A daughter denying Robert Castle's command would have had to have been a humiliating surprise for a person of his perceived stature. But later, when society and title and wealth are beginning to mean less, does he miss her? Was there ever regret? Or reconciliation?

"Wow, you know a lot about a casual acquaintance," John, says, attempting a smile.

Crimson already coloring Jess's cheeks is obviously the first response to the not so subtle comment. Then, with no need for embarrassment, he follows up with clarification: "Mabel's pretty, so she expects to be pursued. I figured, why not take a chance on asking? So I did, and she politely agreed to an ice cream in Far Rockaway Park. It was there on a bench that she did most all the talking."

"And…?" John had to ask.

"I never saw her again. I tried at first, rang her up, but seemed to always get the party line people. It soon became clear to me she had no interest so then neither did I.

"You know what, though, I remember now that she said she had had to give up her beautiful baby grand piano that Dada, the name for their father, had given her because of her pure soprano voice and talent for the piano.

"'He was brokenhearted, and never recovered from the depression of the Depression,' she said. I felt bad for her," Jess says.

"The musical talent doesn't surprise me. I had a feeling she played," John says. It makes him happy to know they share an interest in music. "So I guess you've got your answer, Jess, as to whether the family is still wealthy."

"Yeah, guess so. But they could still have money: look, they have stayed in that big house out there on Doughty Boulevard. That says something."

"You mean you know where her family lives?" This was getting better all the time.

"Yeah, that's right, I forgot: Crowell asked me to pick her up one morning when she'd stayed overnight at home and had to get to work for the early shift—and no buses were running at the right time. Once again she seemed nice, no signs of living up to her gossip line reputation. She was appreciative, not haughty."

"Jess, if she isn't at work today, would you mind directing me to her home?"

"Man, you don't listen, do you? But, okay, will do. I'm just warning you you're barking up the wrong tree. She'd never be interested in an ordinary average guy. Look at me: one of her many discards. She goes for upscale boyfriends, so you'll only get hurt." Jess's efforts are useless. He means well, but has no way to know the depth of his partner's emotion.

#

"Hi there, fellas," Crowell says, smiling her typical hearty welcome that includes reaching for a hug. "Good trip I hope." And sensing John's singular interest, the question already forming on his lips, she preempts with, "Off duty today, I'm afraid. She's been planning to take some days off to be with her family for something, and it's this week," she says sadly.

Against better judgment, the very judgment that had prevented her from her silly idea to introduce John to Mabel in absentia somehow, Crowell follows instinct:

"But I bet you can find her at home."

John practically drags Jess away from his friends, the old crowd he'd worked with. A promise is a promise, and John needs a navigator. They have already unloaded the children and know they are in good hands. John hurries with the paperwork while Jess takes care of loose ends. It's down to counting minutes, not hours or months or years anymore. This is it: he and Jess are on their way to Inwood and the big house on the boulevard. Crowell had no idea that the Castle family had moved into temporary quarters while the homestead was being remodeled into a two-family, complete with new wallpaper and paint throughout. Mabel had taken time off work to share in the packing and other duties with her siblings.

As soon as Jess ordered, "Stop, this is it," John could see he faced another brick wall, this time literally. The red-brick and brown-shingled exterior with its tan porch shedding original paint was obviously under renovation, deserted except for the building crew and a couple of painters.

"No! No more bad news, please!" Unusual for John but understandable. Dejected for only a moment, John jumps out of the car and runs up to the porch.

"Excuse me, I'm looking for the Castle fam…."

He couldn't finish before the laughter: "This here ain't no castle, mister, and there ain't no king or queen inside." The guy was tired near the end of his labor and a bit giddy. Then he tried to help: "Hey, Tony, come mere, [sic] over by the stairs. You know where they went, them [sic] people that live here? Okay, so how about you, Richie: you know where they are? Nobody's got a clue? How about Carl over there? You, yes you, do you know where the people are?" With another no, the first man turns back to John. "Sorry, mister, we don't know about the people. We're just workers: they don't tell us nothing [sic]."

John offers a handshake of thanks and walks back to the van. By now he is exhausted from the assault on his soul and the sounds of construction. It is almost too much for him this time: too many years of disappointment. He has come so far and finds only another impasse. He had believed fervently that she was within reach this time. It is devastating.

They drive back upstate in silence, Jess at the wheel, John in sorrow. It's clear he has nothing to say. But Jess does: looking straight ahead he stretches his arm over to his buddy and places his hand on his shoulder, an attempt to show he cares and supports him, and to encourage him with these carefully considered words:

"John, don't take everything I said today to heart. If any man stands a chance with her, I really think you're that man."

"Thanks, Jess. I needed that. I was actually beginning to believe it myself, but I guess I just have a bad case of wishful thinking."

"No. Give it some time," Jess gently suggests. He has no idea how comical that sounds. He is simply glad to see, quickly, with eyes on the road of course—John smiling now, almost laughing.

#

Soon smiling turns to meditation. Johnny goes deeper inside himself, even confronting God.

"Father, why, why are you doing so much to prevent my even meet-
ing Mabel? Are you testing me? Do you really doubt my sincerity?
I thought you were a knowing God. And I still do; it's just that my
patience has run out of faith. I'm sorry. All right then, I'll keep on. If
that's what you want, I'll prove myself to you. I'll work around your
detours, stumble through your maze, and show more willingness to
wait. I'm an expert in it. So I will be patient. I will wait to see what
you have in store for me instead of trying to direct the outcome
myself. Forgive me for being so self-willed. Thy will, not mine, be
done. In Jesus' name. Amen."

In the semi-silence of confronting God in prayer, John has questioned, agreed, promised, and ended with a plea for forgiveness. He didn't mind that his friend was sitting right beside him in the truck. He's sure Jess was concentrating solely on safe driving and didn't hear a word. Later, there is no doubt who did.

#

It began with a break from routine. There would be a mid-year transfer of children to Wave Crest for the cheer of holiday season celebration and a study of its viability for a permanent place on the winter calendar. John was asked to do the transfer, and he agreed on the spot. Years earlier it had been his duty, though happily, but now it is his privilege. All of a sudden he is filled with Christmas spirit, the impetus for one more try at love. They leave early the next day.

After the orderlies receive and settle the patients, and John completes his paperwork, he walks around the building and enters by way of the main lobby. Immediately a huge evergreen Christmas tree demands attention, standing proud in the far corner of the Great Room, not yet adorned, just beautifully raw, and perfumed by pine. Someone is playing Christmas carols on the piano and he peeks into the small music room to see if it might be Mabel. It is not. Within minutes Crowell comes bounding down the stairs and they hug each other in a way that only Christmas brings about. He is alone this time: not enough children were able to make the winter trip, so no need for an assistant. Crowell, too old, too wise, and too caring to procrastinate on something so important as love, is suddenly unable to broach the subject, their subject, with John who waits expectantly, his eyes seeking hers for an answer as they stand opposite each other.

Be direct! It's your obligation, her conscience directs. He deserves to be told. Go on!

"She's not here, John," she blurts out fast before tears. But her forever-sensitive soul still feels his disappointment as acutely as if it were her own. And God help her, there's more:

"Mabel resigned two weeks ago."

The words stung: and as they registered, the young man's face turned ashen, aging in place. Pain engraved. Crowell stands alone, feeling powerless to help.

Or is she…?

No, she's not helpless. She has just found her way. "But we're having a party here for her tonight. Sort of a farewell send-off and Christmas Ball combined. Even a band. It promises to be fun. I'd like you to stay, John, and enjoy it with us."

What Crowell doesn't know is that it is to be an engagement party as well. Mabel intends to announce her betrothal and introduce the man she is to marry, Russell Gordon of New Jersey. They met several years ago at a family camp retreat in the mountains. It is where their father took his girls for several summers to wait tables and learn Biblical tenets. And where a strong friendship developed between Mabel and Russell that continued from a distance for quite some time, and eventually turned serious with a marriage proposal. Mr. and Mrs. Castle, Alfred and Ella, are delighted with their daughter's decision. Russell comes from a well-connected country club family, follows the same faith, and will be a good provider. Mabel will live in a culture of enviable wealth and be happy ever after.

#

John hesitates, wanting to accept the party invitation and wanting also to avoid it. He can see himself standing alone, wall flower, watching people that already know to each other as friends, family, or coworkers eager to celebrate together. And can he even afford the time, or more important, anymore hurt to his heart?

"I'm sure it will be all right if you stay over—I'll prepare one of the orderly rooms for you—and you can drive back tomorrow," Crowell says. "Being the Christmas season and all. In fact, I'd be happy to call Margaret and tell her myself."

Crowell sure is convincing. But why not stay? Brighten up for Christmas. There's nothing more to lose, John realizes.

"Yes, I accept your invitation," he says. "Thanks, Crowell. And I'll speak to the Eckards when you call, if you don't mind."

They had a short but cordial conversation, after which John hurried over to Central Avenue to shop for his first formal suit. And Crowell makes still another call.

"Hello dear, just calling to confirm that your parents plan to be at the party tonight. Your sisters? How nice it will be to see them. I look forward to it. It is going to be a grand evening.

"Oh, by the way Mabel, I...I want to tell you there's going to be someone new with us tonight. Someone who would like to meet you. What? Oh, just a good friend of mine. See you later, my dear."

Interlude

She seems to be walking on air, floating, looking every bit the vision he's held close to his heart all these years. Dressed in winter white velvet, the gown cut to perfection with a modest sweetheart neckline, curls piled high atop her head, she is radiant. Angelic. Heaven sent. Yes, it had been God listening in. John watched her every move, graceful and gliding around the room, extending her hand to a host of familiar faces. She is holding court it looks like, and he is witnessing nothing less than a princess at play.

And of the many people surrounding her he feels blessed to be so near. He has eyes only for her: Following. Penetrating. Inviting. Then, in what can only be defined as a magical moment, Mabel happens to look his way. And stops: suspended in mid-sentence. A flashback. The kitchen. Years ago. A hot summer afternoon with Bertha, drinking a cola … both admiring the good-looking man recumbent against the icebox, magnetic eyes searching hers before she turned away. And now those eyes are speaking, and she isn't turning from them. Immediately she knows: there is no need to question Crowell. He is of whom she spoke, the friend who wants to meet her. She doesn't understand it all, why he's there, alone, and in uncomfortable timing, but she knows intuitively she must meet him too.

And they walk toward each other, the band playing soft Crosby, the room full of people in clusters, involved in separate little worlds of their own, as they, Mabel and John, enter theirs. Without even a word she takes the hand he offers and walks into his arms. He's never danced before but it feels natural. So do the lyrics in the band's beautiful interpretation of the new hit, "I'm in the Mood for Love," as Crowell, directly across the floor, moves quickly to a powder room, just minutes ahead of her tears. She has been standing behind the refreshment table, dressed in her very finest, waiting for just such an encounter. They had not needed her introduction. She wanted to see them, but be unnoticed at a distance when they met, hoping the compelling young man would find it to be all he had waited for. She cares nothing about that other one she's never met, and hopes never will. Mabel deserves the best. All of a sudden she is perfect for John in Crowell's eyes. And all is fair in love and war she believes: by gosh, this poor man has been fighting a battle just to get close to the front line!

"I'm Mabel."

"I know. I'm John."

"I remember."

"I'm not sure I understand.…"

"The day in the kitchen … many years ago when you walked in for a drink. It came back to me as soon as I saw you standing over there."

"I've been looking for you."

"Well, I've been here ever since." She looks puzzled, wondering just how hard he had tried.

"Ah, but I haven't."

And he explains that he lives and works upstate. Then to his surprise, he quickly adds that he will be moving down this way sometime after the first of the year. "I'm finished with academics, also my car"— no time to explain — "and there are much better job opportunities here on the island."

And to her own surprise, she realizes she has just turned her new diamond ring around to hide its sparkle. From "Smoke Gets in Your Eyes," John's favorite, to "My Happiness," evident in both, they hold tight to each other, neither wanting to let go, both knowing they must, and soon. She broke the spell first.

"I should return to my family and guest now." Biting her lip to stop a smile, she is secretly amused by her description of Russell. Until moments ago she had intended to gather her friends and families—the Castles, the Gordons, church members, Wave Crest coworkers—and take the stage to announce her engagement and introduce her fiancée.

"Thank you, Mabel." John means for far more than the dances. Her eyes, her honesty, her sense of ease with him verified he has not been a fool.

No answer in the etiquette books for this. What is the proper thing to do? Mabel doesn't want to leave him, interrupt the magic of the moment, and yet she has an obligation.

"It was so nice meeting you, John, and dancing with you. Glad you were able to be here tonight. Maybe later I can, or maybe you would like to … to talk again, well … if…." She is struggling. And he rescues. Instinctively he knows her guest is her escort. He is, most likely, the man watching them now, as he'd been for most of their time together. John does not want Mabel to be uncomfortable all evening. He's feeling very generous at that moment. His time will come. "If we don't get a chance to talk again, Mabel, may I write to you?"

"Oh, that would be wonderful," she says excitedly, then quickly catches herself. "I mean, yes, of course."

It is only her first step away when she turns and looks back over her shoulder, coyly adding: "Or call. Crowell has the number." Then a sweet smile and she's gone.

#

A mother always knows. It's the genes talking. From little girl to young woman to last days, there is in us silent dialogue more potent than language and song, with presence only as aura. And Mabel has been wrapped in it all evening.

"Who was that rather dashing young fellow you spoke with, darling?" Ella Castle pleasantly asks in past tense, ignoring the subject of inappropriate dances as she pours her daughter punch and attempts a smile that tells another story. Same for her soldier-march posture, meant to be regal and far removed from the elephant. She tries so hard to appear unconcerned and accepting, but her manner speaks fear. It will not do to upset Russell—this is one match the matriarch definitely wants to happen. She's been an advocate for the cause for years. Right now she desperately needs to scold her daughter, shame her for flirting, for showing disrespect to a fiancé not properly acknowledged yet, though secretly expected to be later tonight. Now her daughter's defiance suggests delay. The unraveling of perfect plans is almost too much for a concerned mother to watch. Of course she says nothing, consciously that is: just gently guides Mabel over to her father and Russell who are busy impressing each other as they discuss the condition of the dollar. Ella's question remains unanswered, as intended. She hadn't wanted a response. Her message was in the asking.

"Lovely evening isn't it, sweetheart?" Alfred says, opening his arms to Mabel.

"Oh, yes dear father, and I am so happy that you and Mama and my sisters are here with me tonight as I say good-bye to Wave Crest."

Alfred is in his glory this evening: a gregarious personality who loves a party as much as the stage. With handsomely etched high cheekbones and silver grey hair, he's often the star of the church play circuit, popular entertainment of that era. Friendships, exposure, contacts are made that way, he often says. He is also active in the spiritual life of his church, St. Paul's Methodist in Inwood, and believes in the importance of fellowship. Watching Mabel and Russell join others on the crowded dance floor, the father remarks with pride: "They certainly do make a handsome couple."

He, too, is very pleased with his daughter's choice. Russell will be a good provider and life partner, he hopes, like the kind and generous always smiling young man Edith is blessed to have married: Lewis Jackson, a devout believer born with musical gifts for the church. Mary married Corty Wood—entertainer at heart, joining Alfred in plays made popular by their harmony—but a serious businessman as well. It is left to the son, Fred, younger than his sisters, to carry on the Castle name. He already has his eye on Kathleen Keen, but she's quite a bit younger and not ready to get serious. There will be resistance from her twin brother and entire Catholic family, but ultimately she follows her heart and they do marry.

"I say, my love, aren't you listening?" Alfred asks his wife. "Don't our Mabel and Russell make a splendid couple?"

"I hope so." And that's all she could say.

"Happy, my sweet one?" Russell asks Mabel with zero-degree interest and hidden disgust. He is not about to give any power to the encounter he witnessed across the room that has his blood still boiling. No, he will certainly not fan the fire. He would prefer to slap her, admonish her for such disloyal behavior, tell her no woman, fiancé or wife, does that to Russell Gordon. But there will be time to set her straight later.

"So when do we make our announcement, my sweet? Shall I have the band do an intro, ask the drummer to heighten the suspense?" he asks her so she can tell him what he already knows. That it will not be tonight.

"Russell, I've decided this isn't the right time, or place really, to make such an announcement. This is a Christmas Ball, and a farewell to me too, but only as a quick, 'We'll miss you,' or something like that. The night belongs to everyone. After all, it is an annual Wave Crest event; it just doesn't seem proper to tag on a formal engagement announcement. I'd rather have my parents plan a small party specifically for us, for that one purpose. We'll do it soon."

There it is. Done. Thank goodness. Mabel is relieved and especially pleased with herself that she could hide behind those words so well. What came out had actually made sense. But what couldn't come out is what bothers her: feelings, never like this for Russell, unexplainable, but strong and unavoidable, are swimming inside her, circling her heart. She fears she is about to ride alone the rough waves of high-tide emotion.

#

The shiny black roadster purrs as it travels down the familiar highway, and John's pride of accomplishment is riding high. So is his sense of urgency as he makes his first personal trip to Wave Crest for a visit with Mabel, by invitation.

There are only a few days until Christmas. He'd written to her, and her answer was protocol prompt. It was she who asked if they might see each other before the holiday week. If he arrives early enough, they'll go to dinner tonight, a Friday. They both have Saturday and most of Sunday free which seems perfectly planned from above. Mabel is officially back on staff now, assigned the same room she'd shared with Alva after they both were promoted and given coveted semiprivate quarters, but not scheduled for duty until Monday, courtesy of Crowell. Her family doesn't know yet, and may not even wonder about her weekend absence, unless "an emergency request for additional help" at Wave Crest" occurs. Crowell has no problem with 'exaggeration' if it benefits love. And her romantic antenna is sensitive to the urgency of this meeting. Russell is due to arrive from New Jersey early Christmas Eve. Crowell has arranged for John to share a room with one of the orderlies, as she had once before, making it possible for Mabel and John to have quality time together. It took her innate foresight and fast affection for a young man, combined with a favorite young nurse, to see the beauty of intuition at work.

"It's late, is there a restaurant still open?" he, the man with no appetite, asks as they prepare for their run to the car—ducking the unexpected hail and cutting short their visit with Crowell who'd been waiting with Mabel in the reception room.

Crowell certainly didn't mind the long hours waiting for John. She works well with Cupid.

"Yes, down on Central Avenue, next to the cinema there's a cozy little place that stays open to catch the movie theatre crowd," Crowell tells them.

John puts his jacket over Mabel and helps her into the car, then goes around to his side and as he climbs in she says, "I love your car."

And I love you, he thinks but answers, "Thanks. I built it."

"How does one build a car?" She is already impressed.

"It begins with need, a very motivating factor." He was half kidding. "Then it takes proximity to a junk yard, not only for the basic parts but for all the mysteries you uncover as you go along; the little extra pieces you have to run back and search for. It takes persistence. And patience."

"And talent." Stated emphatically by his newest fan. "I think you're brilliant," she says.

Like your eyes, he thinks, but answers only, "No, not at all, but thank you."

All through dinner they study each other, learning how much alike they are. John wants to follow impulse and reach over to kiss her, but he knows better. Yet it would have seemed so right: a natural move. He feels at home with her already.

Mabel's questions reveal her genuine interest, a caring desire to know him, yet she handles it with class, keeping within proper boundaries. What he shares, she gladly accepts. And he finds himself telling her more than he's ever told anyone before.

She is easy to talk to. She is enchanting. Endearing. And even more:

compassionate and beautiful inside. He asks about her, also with good taste, and she answers openly. But she is stunned by his story. It touched her heart. And once, when he is telling about his father's last hours, she leans across the table and takes his hand, leaving hers to rest upon, hand over hand as one. Fire finding fire.

"We'll locate them, Johnny. I know your aunt and uncle are out there somewhere; I just know it. And they're probably looking for you. I bet they're not even very far away. I'll help you find them, Johnny. Really. I think it would be fascinating; I really want to. I'd love to help. It can be our little, our own, um, project. That's it. Our project. Together."

So moved was she that she inadvertently crossed the invisible line drawn earlier whereby she warned herself not to expect too much, nor promise too much….

"Well, I don't worry about it anymore, Mabel. I don't dwell on it, not to the extent I did as a kid anyway. When I was young I guess I was obsessed about the unfairness. Now I give it very little thought. My priorities have changed. But, of course, deep down there still is a part of me that would like to reach out, to link up with my heritage. Sort of a bloodline desire to connect, I suppose.

"It means a lot, what you just said to me, Mabel. Yes, I think I'll hold you to your word. It's nice to know you want to help. I've never really thought anyone would care about that part of my life. I've always considered myself too subjective in that regard. How would it interest anyone else? So thanks. It feels good to think of someone wanting to share in my search," John says.

"I care," she says.

And he trusts that to be true.

The weekend gives credence to the bond that for her began on a dance floor, for him in a kitchen, and they are like two children experiencing for the first time the wonders of a day at the fair. On Saturday they take a short drive and walk, hand in hand, through a veil of snowflakes in a deserted park. They went window shopping and each slipped away to buy the other a gift: she a pocket-size toolbox ideally suited to his car, "For the man who can fix anything"; and he a copper-dipped maple-leaf brooch that reads, "Penny for Your Thoughts." She wouldn't disclose them just then but promised they were happy ones.

They climb a narrow stairwell, the only light a collection of lanterns to lead the way until they reach the recommended "best ever" Chinese restaurant where they linger over dinner and tea for hours, lulled by chimes touching softly above. It is a lovely respite from the busy, sometimes pushy, holiday shoppers along Central Avenue below. They feel far removed and joyously alone, sitting side by side now. And in that darkened mezzanine mood, John allows himself for the first time the ease of simply putting his arm around the woman at his side.

Afterward they return to Wave Crest and sit by the almost-to-ceiling Christmas tree now fully and exquisitely decorated with fragile Victorian ornaments. Had they even noticed it as they danced by at the ball? Its beauty fills the room and showcases the delicate art on the tree and the sway of flames in both fireplaces. It's mesmerizing. They're not talking, not needing to: drinking in instead the presence of the other. Sunday after brunch, they walk along the beach, bundled up against the cold wind, knowing that all too soon their idyllic weekend will be over. It was there, then, at that very moment, that John took Mabel in his arms, cuddling her trembling body, shielding her against the elements, and finally bending to kiss her.

Oh, how he'd longed for this moment. Not even the harsh wind blowing off the sea can chill the fire of his passion. And she returns his kisses with similar intensity, kissing his eyes, his cheeks, his neck, his lips again. And again. John, pulling her still closer to his body, is no longer standing at water's edge but rather deep in the center of euphoria, the middle of a dream, embraced by a feeling of serenity he's never before experienced. Today he is beginning to learn how it feels to not be alone. They release each other and walk slowly back over the sand dunes to the main house warmed by the knowledge that nothing is ending but instead has only just begun.

CHAPTER XV

She walks up to the porch steps alone. It was going to be difficult. Confrontation always is. "I've come home to discuss something very important with you, Mother, Dada. Please hear me out." Mabel looks first to her father, then her mother, beseeching them to understand. They had accepted the fact, begrudgingly, that she was postponing the engagement and returning to her job at the hospital. She had said there would be time to plan a lavish wedding later. Now she is about to further disappoint with words her mother already knows.

"There will be no wedding after all. Ever. I'm sorry. I just can't marry Russel. When he comes down this weekend, I will be returning the ring. No, please, Mother, wait.

"I know now that I don't love Russell. Not the way I've always hoped to love a man. For a while I was willing to settle for the symbiotic marriage it would be, thinking that was enough. But I've discovered recently that there is much more. There's a kind of love, romantic and real, that does exist, and I want nothing less for myself." She paused and said, "And I have found that now. Please be happy for me."

"I knew it! It's that John what's-his-name, isn't it? I knew it!" says Ella Castle with unknown anger. "That ambulance driver who appeared out of nowhere, unannounced and uninvited, at the Christmas Ball and filled your head with nonsense. It's him, right?" She was losing control. "Admit it," she orders. "What's gotten into you, Mabel? You used to be so sensible.

Why now, after years of waiting, would you throw away a life like Russell has offered you? What can this other fellow ever give you? Nothing I tell you, just mediocrity, if that. And an ethnic surname! What promises has he been feeding you?"

The mother's hostility stings. Mabel wants so much for her mother, and her father, good man to a good man, to approve and welcome warmly her beloved John. She wonders how her mother even knew his name. She'd been careful to keep her growing relationship a secret.

"First of all, Johnny is not just a driver," Mabel says. "He finished with honors at a two-year college all on his own and is very talented in anything electrical and mechanical, and is just very smart. He has a new job as head mechanic at the Lincoln Cadillac dealership, and can you imagine, he actually built his own car without any help?"

"A mechanic?" It was Alfred in shock this time.

"No, Father. A man. First and foremost a very fine man, with many of the qualities I've always admired in you: integrity, kindness, strength, and ambition. A daughter learns that from her father and looks for it in a husband."

"Oh, no!" Ella wails on her way to the floor in readiness of a fainting spell that fails. Aware of her mother's occasional histrionics, Mabel continues. It is so important to her that her parents understand.

"John has so much kindness and love to give. I wish you could know him, Mother, Dada, because you would be proud to have him as a son."

"We have a son, thank you," Ella says.

Mabel knows already that John would be different from her father who shows only minimal affection to his children and obvious partiality of which she is recipient, and that saddens her, though she never mentions it. Instead she conceals that truth and continues the conversation ...

"And by the way, John is a self-made man. Everything he has accomplished he has done all alone: there was never any family behind him."

"That's just the point!" charges the mother. "No family! What do you know about him, with no background? What's he hiding? What's in his blood? Would you want your children to have a questionable lineage?" So upset and outraged by her daughter's mistake-in-the-making, Ella leaves the room. They'd been in the kitchen, usually the happiest room in the house, but now it's ugly in its aftermath of anger.

"I'll make some tea, Dada," Mabel says.

"Yes, thank you. We'll take it in the dining room. Would there be any of your mother's little pastries left in the cupboard, do you think? If so, I shall indulge. Just one, though; I know you have a liking for them as well."

With mild compassion but calculated manipulation, Alfred Castle chose the road of less resistance for continuing the delicate dialog with his daughter. She was the spirited child, deliberate, and delightful he thought to himself as he watched her now, sitting so composed, a beautiful young woman caught up in the mysteries of love. He's giving her some quiet time and little reason to rebel. Opposition would only make her more defensive. So when their respite ends, Alfred proceeds with caution.

"Mabel, you know I want only your happiness. I recognize that ultimately it is up to you to decide where that happiness may lie. I ask only that you be patient with yourself: weigh your feelings carefully. It all happened so fast. Don't break your engagement prematurely. Give equal time to both young men so that you can be very sure."

Her eyes told him she didn't agree. She'd feel like a hypocrite: it just wouldn't be fair.

"I'm not asking you to be deceitful, darling. Instead, it's really an act of' honesty for finding truth." He is playing to her strong convictions.

"Don't you see? It would be disastrously unfair to Russell to abruptly cancel plans you've spent years engineering. Now don't look so innocent. You know you've been actively charming the man for quite some time. You led him to believe you wanted nothing else than to be his wife. His ring was in response to those subtleties. So you can't just drop an established relationship because another attractive man displays an interest in you.

"You will always draw attention, Mabel: men react favorably to you. You are lovely, if I may say so as a proud father. Certainly you won't spend a lifetime following each flattering encounter. You must learn to live with it and see a man's folly for what it is. Stay true to your goals, your purpose, your own best interests," Alfred says, sounding rather wise to his daughter all of a sudden. He watched her, wanting to make sure he didn't hit too hard, so as to insult or bore her and drive her away before she has a chance to absorb his words. "You must test this attraction, this man's quick interest and dare I say, pressure. Make sure the interest is sincere; that his motives are pure. And most of all, that what you are feeling is real. Just remember, you always did like romantic drama—Mr. Darcy and other Austen residents are still on your shelf. Keep that in mind.

"All I'm really saying is be careful, go easy on yourself, unhurried in making a life-changing decision; and that when you do, it is based on what is best for you in the long run. You're young: there's no rush. If this man, John, really loves you he'll wait."

She knew that to be true. He'd waited so long already. But maybe everything else Dada is saying is true too, she's thinking. He is a wise man and his counsel has served her well throughout her life. She should probably follow it again.

"Would you like me to warm your tea, Dada?"

"No thank you, dear, but perhaps another petit four?" And she goes back into the kitchen, returning with the very last miniature sweet cake. She watches her father enjoy a second forbidden pastry, noticing age on his brow and the silver strands in his hair. It is unsettling, though she doesn't exactly know why. She has just felt a surge of love for him. She walks around to his chair opposite hers at the elongated Windsor dining table that owns the room and sits down on her father's lap to hug his neck.

"I love you, Dada." She hugs him a minute and then adds the gift of words he has prayed to hear: "I know that you are right in all you've said this afternoon, and I will do what you say. I won't stop seeing John, because it's a comparison still, but I will keep it a friendship and be honest with him about still seeing Russell." It was important for Mabel to qualify that. She knew she couldn't allow herself two suitors. "So I guess I won't end my engagement," she says to her father already worrying about her hesitation. She is thinking about Russell, how they have begun to drift apart, and he hasn't even noticed.

"Russell Gordon is so busy with his business dealings right now, Dada, I doubt he's paid any attention to the increasing length of time between our visits. I haven't even seen him since the Christmas Ball."

"Well, when is it that you will see him again?" Alfred is anxious for progress. "Surely he will be here for Christmas Eve service, right?"

"I think so. I'm not sure anymore. But I think so. And I've been invited to Montclair for Regina's welcome home dinner party in January. You remember his sister, right?"

"Yes, of course I do. Lovely young woman," he says.

"Well, she is returning from Europe where she has been studying art. Now she will be involved with the Works Progress Administration's Federal Art Project producing sculptures. She's quite good, you know."

"How timely, Mabel. It will be a nice opportunity for you to blend in as family instead of feeling like a guest. The Gordons are gracious hosts. Your mother and I so enjoyed the Thanksgiving holiday with them. Please don't forget to give them our regards." And with a twinkle in his eye and a subdued smile of victory, he adds, "And you'll give them your best. Right, Mabel? Purge the other thoughts from your mind when you are with them. Be fair to Russell, and to yourself too."

She nods in agreement.

Alfred thinks ahead to the annual Bible Conference compound in the mountains of Northern New Jersey where he and most of his family still participate, and he sees it as a good tool this year. The retreat has always been a boost to his daughter's long distance relationship, a perfect place to rekindle romantic feelings and plan for a life together. And now with that official ring on her finger, it should accelerate the process. The father is already looking forward to late summer when free of other persuasion. Mabel and Russell will be there renewing their love and commitment. And perhaps even setting a definite wedding date: initial preparations have long been poised to zoom into high gear. Yes, it will be a happy spring and summer ... as long as early opposing thoughts don't linger in Mabel's head. Or heart.

Alfred Castle is satisfied that he has averted tragedy, and it shows like the broad smile of a champion as arm in arm, father and daughter leave the room. Her father's words play over and over in her head, and Mabel is convinced he has spoken sensibly. Her dilemma is she just can't reconcile herself to continuing to see John while engaged to another. A moral woman doesn't do that. She has an allegiance to Russell until she decides otherwise.

In the beginning it was new, a surprise that took her off guard and swept her away, engulfing her in newfound happiness. Seeing John seemed permissible because in her heart of hearts she believed she would be ending her relationship with Russell.

Of course, now it's different. She has chosen a sober approach. She has chosen her father. To see John under these new conditions would be to betray him. She won't do that. How could she tell him that in two weeks she'll be off to visit her future in-laws? Or bid farewell to one man and be welcomed by the other? And allow to be kissed at arrival when having been embraced at departure? Oh, no. It would be so cruel to have to say, "Sorry, I'm off to my annual month in the mountains where I shall be seeing Russell almost every day. No, there is no kind way out. The only fair thing is to put it on hold: tell John she is engaged. He never knew that. She never announced it. And she had turned the ring so that its sparkle wouldn't show. She wishes she could put it back in the little velvet box for a rest, absent while the requisite Christmas occasions and expectations are satisfied and her confusion quiets into calm and clear for the New Year. But the ring has to be worn during the holiday season whenever Russell is in the house and thereabout—for his own appreciation and, of course, the Gordon family pride. Her head is spinning, her ring rash itching, and she happens to be thinking only of John, and how to soften the hurt.

"Oh, this is awful: I'm so confused. I feel phony, like a liar," Mabel laments to her frayed, but precious still, teddy bear for its comfort of yesteryear. Her confidant, Alva, is off this weekend, just when Mabel needs her perspective. She says her prayers, asking for guidance, then falls into a tortured sleep.

#

Crowell hands Johnny the letter. He has just arrived in 'their' roadster, expecting to catch Mabel coming off duty. Instead an envelope takes her place. And the fact that Crowell stands stoic instead of her usual welcome with a hug means it probably contains a message of doom.

So he says goodbye, he'll be heading out, and Crowell counters: "You might want to come back later and have some coffee and maybe a little conversation, Johnny. I'll be here till 11:00 or later tonight. Love you," she says and quickly and disappears.

"Well, that's a first," John mumbles on his way to the car. He has to get away and read the ruling in private.

Dear Johnny:

Please try to understand and forgive. I have not been completely fair to you and I can no longer continue this way. Russell is still a part of my life, and I must return to that life now. In not being fair to you, I also have not been true to him. Or maybe most of all, I have not been true to myself. I am reinstated at Wave Crest, a seamless return to work. I shall be thinking about you, wishing you well always. I ask, however, that you do not try to contact me.

Sincerely, Mabel

He puts the note on the leather seat beside him, where she belongs, and rubs his eyes. It is so hard to understand, so unexpected, so devastating. Dreams don't usually last long, and he knows that. They're like balloons, or ethereal clouds: their brevity bemoaned, and in rare cases painful. This is rare. John is hurting as he takes back the note and folds it—no, compresses it: his palms taking the pain—into a capsule that might as well be a bullet. He puts the pellet into his shirt pocket and starts the car. The single one person who could alleviate the physical pain burning in his core and comfort him is, of course, the very one who has caused the wound. His next trusted friend is Crowell, so he accepts her offer to return and slowly walks back inside. He can smell the freshness of the just-brewed coffee that Crowell expected would be needed, and he is thankful for her friendship. She pours for two. His face tells her what the letter says. But by its very existence, she already knows the contents. He did not offer to share the actual note because of its condition, and also because he feels it's impolite to pass correspondence beyond its intended recipient. Crowell understands his protective posture, and feels sure Mabel would have written in a kind and careful, but deliberate, tone. It would not have been an easy letter for her to compose. No frills, of course: just short and to the point. There was not much to say. John is there for comfort, not analysis. And Crowell tries her best to console him, but how do you undo agony? She isn't completely convinced that Mabel is fully convinced, knowing her so well. She wants to give John a few words of encouragement before they part. Because something has happened to redirect the trajectory of love, a startling change of heart, and it suggests to Crowell interference from the parents. If so, Mabel might begin to doubt herself. When they finish looking for happy subjects that seldom help in sorrow, they stand to say goodbye, and as Crowell tightly holds John in a hug, she whispers in his ear: "Give the girl a little time, Johnny."

CHAPTER XVI

Holiday season now packed away, Mabel and Russell are together for a weekend at the Gordon family home. They have discussed and survived what Russell called a "one-time only unfortunate display" and were back on track to the altar. The home is exquisite, a Windsor Castle West. The spirit of eighteenth-century England floats through the rooms, the most impressive being the dining room, bookended by handsome wood-burning fireplaces and filled with Chippendale mahogany revivals. The intricately carved-at-the-corners of an oblong table with accompanying high-back chairs are decorated in a reduced matching pattern and seat eighteen; again, Chippendale. Heavy floor-length draperies deep in the hues of ruby-red satin warm the room as well as cover the windows. And the oversized crystal silver-touched chandelier, positioned to reflect the brilliance of silver candelabra placed at each end of the table, finalizes Mrs. Gordon's goal. As the butler serves crème Brulee with an addition of fresh fruit, Regina completes her lengthy monologue of student life at the Sorbonne, and conversation quickly turns to Russell and Mabel.

"Obviously we've passed the opportunity of a winter wedding, and actually a spring, summer and fall as well," Millicent Gordon says. "We don't want to just throw something together: we want to make a statement." Mrs. Gordon is a proud woman, artistic and very organized: her only son's wedding must be presented as an event. She intends to oversee every detail important to the preparation of perfection and will generously subsidize over budget upscale costs. Although protocol clearly puts the responsibility of a wedding on the bride's family, it means nothing to the mother of this groom. She expects to be in charge. That has always been her role. Frankly, though, she's beginning to feel uneasy about Mabel to say the least: without any warning or logic, Mabel alone postponed the engagement announcement and now seems to be lacking in interest, not to mention enthusiasm.

"Don't you agree, Mabel? Nothing but the best for your wedding?"

But before Mabel could even form an answer, Millicent spoke again: "Precisely when may we expect this long-awaited occasion?" she asks with definite sarcasm. "There's a lot to do to plan a wedding. I'd at least like a timeframe as soon as you can provide me one."

"Of course," Mabel says, having no real answer except that it will be as initially planned: about a year and a half away. "I was thinking, Mrs. Gordon, that late this summer we could formally announce the engagement in the press with a firm date for the wedding the following June. It is considered to be the best month for summer weddings; I guess because the sun's not quite as unbearable as mid August. Or do you think a spring wedding in May would be best?

"No, let's stay in June" Millicent says. "We can easily get around the sun situation by an early evening wedding, say like 6:00 PM, a really formal hour after sunset. Yes, I think it could be a regal presentation. The chapel is significantly smaller than our church, requiring trimming down the guest list. But in the spirit of serendipity there is this: exclusivity. Survivors of the cut become elitist, and are envied for their invitation to attend the late-day wedding party." Millicent is pleased with the tradeoff; though its balance is not hers to claim.

"But going with June accelerates everything," Mabel says. ""Definitely we will have to begin very soon to make it happen: reservations for upscale establishments may already be difficult to secure," she continues, beginning to sound a little too much like Mrs. Gordon, she fears."

"You and I will have a lot of time in the interim to shop and put plans in place for a beautiful ceremony and scrumptious dinner to follow; also to enjoy the usual bridal shower, luncheons, and requisite garden party tea that are part of a proper wedding," she adds. She is trying to appease her future mother-in-law. She is also trying to be true to her father's wishes. And, of course, trying to be considerate of Russell. She isn't in the mix. Nor is John. She is thankful for the days she's taken off from work for herself. It will allow her time to do what her father suggested, although he wants expediency and she, Mabel, wants time alone and honest resolution. Surely, after a year and a half of deliberate time together with the Gordon family, especially the woman most prominent in it, Mabel will have a true picture of her future. What she knows now, though, is that Johnny is gone forever: the decision's over. The length of the "study" Dada proposed prohibits any second-thought opportunity. That ended with her letter. John will soon, if not already, be scooped up by a very wise young woman.

Mabel is glad she sent the letter so that John is free to find a life of love and the children he hopes to have one day.

#

"So, it's June what at six then, Mabel?" Millicent asks, rhetorically. She intends to make her point: "But do we really have to take it out to so far in the future? We still have June of this year. We could have a modified 'event' of the summer in our Country Club. What do you think?"

It takes Mabel a few seconds to leave her last thought, troubled by her new reality: the permanent loss of John.

"Yes, I think so, if you really want a formal affair as the event of the summer season. There's much to be done, as you said." Mabel is confusing the first plan of fully waiting a year and a half with the just hatched hurry-to-a date this coming June, not at all what Mabel has agreed to.

"Okay, good," says the mother-in-law-to-be. "Just as soon as you select the date, you let me know and I will contact Father Dowling. We'll reserve the Rosedale Room at the Country Club and begin tending to myriad absolutes. Of course I know your family is Methodist and we are Episcopalian, but together we are simply believers in the Christian faith. That's what matters. That's where you and Russell met: a Christian conference retreat with no divisions. There should be none now."

Russell and his father have not been paying attention to women talking at the end of the table. It includes Regina who remained silent while the wedding was discussed. She is waiting for a chance to take the stage again. The women finish their church and venue discussion as the men head for brandy and a Cuban cigar in a den designed for just that. Millicent is thinking perhaps she should ask Russell for his ideas. He's fond of posh hotels now and might want to impress the guests with a change from repetitious country club fare. Quickly she rises and reaches out to stop him on his way to join his father in their favorite room for their evening pleasure. But he gets caught in the agenda of his mother. His father has walked on, not wanting to get entangled with female chatter.

"Oh, we've been discussing the wedding, Russell, and I want to include you in the plans of course, darling...."

"Mother, stop: you and Mabel will do a great job in decision making. I defer to you, girls. Anything you want is okay with me," he assures them. "I'm kind of in a hurry: Dad is waiting for me."

"Well," says the mother, "pretty much we have agreed that the wedding will be in New Jersey, Father Dowling officiating...," and Russell scowls, turning immediately to Mabel standing subordinate to Millicent, and asks her: "Is this all right with you?"

But Millicent rudely interrupts: "You agree, dear, that the wedding should be held here in New Jersey, don't you? Didn't we just moments ago discuss the melding of our denominations and that Father Dowling would officiate? We've agreed the location will be our Country Club and the reception hosted therein by our extraordinary staff. That's what I meant when I pulled you into the conversation, Russ. Where would you prefer, our club or a fancy hotel? Think about it." Not waiting for his answer, Millicent continues to coerce her daughter-to-be.

"I mean with so many of our business associates living nearby, Country Club friends, members of our community who have known

Russell ever since he was a baby, well, it just seems easier to manage. You understand, don't you, dear?"

"I guess so. I don't suppose it really matters." Mabel says, beginning to feel like a puppet, all dressed up in pretty princess paint, but a puppet just the same. The question is: Who pulls the strings? Is it Alfred Castle, Millicent Gordon, or Russell?

Right now Russell is the good guy protector. He's about to step in and set some rules. He lives now with an ever-present picture of his humiliation front and center on his mind, and that emboldens him to further dictate the terms of their relationship. "It does matter," Russell says directly to Mabel. "It matters to me because I know it matters to you and your family as much as it does here.

"And let me clarify to both of you right now what I expect as we begin the preparation for our wedding: no assumptions shall be made. Discussions are not decisions. There are only two people with the power to decide in this matter, and I am one of them. We will involve others when appropriate, but nothing should be deemed final or ready for signature without the approval of Mabel or me. And anything agreed to or signed for previously in regard to the wedding is null and void. I should like to be given immediately the date, including year"—even he is not certain—"the time, location of the ceremony and reception, and participating clergy. I will need it now, along with any correspondence related to this endeavor. Cancel immediately anything negotiated in my stead. We're starting over. I expect this is understood?" They smile. He embraces Mabel and whispers, "I trust in whatever you want for our wedding. And please, include your mother in some of the fun stuff."

Mabel is so proud of his loyalty, and indeed feels safe in his arms. Then he leaves to join his father. Millicent and Regina enjoy brandy as well as the men and invite Mable to join them in the formal living room, knowing already that she does not like the taste of after-dinner drinks. She thinks they spoil the taste of a sweet dessert. The occasional butler, Benjamin, has left, so Regina goes to the kitchen and prepares tea for her soon-to-be nubie sister.

#

And when the calendar turns to June of this year, Alfred Castle rejoices. Mabel and Russell are still a happy couple, and staying at the retreat that always enhances their romance. They are involved in some of the social choices as well as enjoying their opportunity to teach: she the youth groups, he the teens. They easily breathed new life into their relationship, as Alfred predicted they would, under a star-filled sky that seems to come very close to touching the Kittatinny Mountains. Dances, careful moonlight walks, picnics, canoe for two almost daily; prayer breakfasts, Bible studies, working with the children—seeing in each other qualities that would ensure a solid marriage. Russell is as adept at persuasion with Mabel as with his colleagues in high stakes finance negotiations.

One evening as they follow the safe-after-dark trail into the woods and settle themselves on a log by a brook feeling so in touch with nature and with each other, Russell begins to speak of their future. The rustic cozy setting mellows Mabel's heart, and when he suggests building a home in the country, in a quaint little town he'd fallen in love with not far from Manhattan—just over the Jersey line—she finds herself agreeing that yes, it would be a perfect place to raise a family.

Chapter XVII

John is building too. Not a family yet, but a career. Sooner than he ever dared to hope, he was actually in business for himself. His talent was too obvious to stay hidden for long and had come to the attention of a loyal Lincoln-Cadillac customer.

"You know, you really ought to be working for yourself, John. It's a waste, fine talent like you working for somebody else. I'm a firm believer in being your own boss when you've got what it takes. And you, young man, have got it." Mr. Lazarus, one of three brothers—*I'm not sure which: I was a child, and he was the revered man in the big house deep in the foliage of Hewlet Bay Park*—in business together as Benrus Watch Company, and had a good eye and big heart. A merchant turned executive, sitting high in the New York sky, he controlled millions of dollars with offices in Switzerland and a lively international trade, so he knows people, and he knows what he wants.

"Thank you. I appreciate what you said about me, Mr. Lazarus. And I've been planning to do that someday. That's why I'm working double shifts now whenever available, to save money to open a business of my own," he tells the gentleman.

"Do it now! Don't wait! Let me give you the money; let me be your benefactor. I'd be honored. I enjoy watching things grow. Buy yourself a string of service stations and you'll be a rich man in no time. That's the way to go." The elder is energized by his idea: he can feel his momentum building. He has missed that thrill.

"I really do intend to follow that path to success someday, as I said. But I just can't let you do it for me, Mr. Lazarus. You're very kind, but I cannot accept your money. Although I will always remember you and be grateful for your gesture."

The praise in itself is priceless to the man of goodwill. Somehow he has to figure this out: the boy, well, young man, is not about to budge. He will have to find a way to make the fellow feel there is no charity involved. A man with pride of purpose, that's what he's dealing with. Plus talent. A winning combination: he better move fast.

"Tell you what, Johnny: let me make you a loan. Whatever it takes, I'll advance you. We will do it fair and square. My lawyers will draw up the papers. Your terms. A loan to you to be paid back in whatever installments you choose." He walks outside to give the guy room to think.

John is stunned by the generosity of opportunity, the once-in-a-lifetime kind, but while it sounds good, it doesn't feel right. And that conflict is evident when Mr. Lazarus returns. He sees John still weighing the offer—grateful, tempted, but not yet ready to accept such a gift when he's not in a position to reciprocate.

"With interest, of course," Mr. Lazarus quickly adds. And that little tag line of fairness becomes the key: John smiles his acceptance.

"You do the legwork. I'm sort of a retiree. I sit back and watch," Mr. Lazarus says.

"Vicarious pleasure." They laughed together: more for relief and happy resolution than appreciation of comedic intent. "Shop around real good," Mr. Lazarus orders. "And when you find what you want, you come to me and we'll work out the details. Better get busy too, 'cause I don't like to be kept waiting. I'll pester you. I am very serious about time, and I want you to be too. Let me hear from you within the week: Progress Report."

"Here's my card." He is about to step into his car, but turns around with a last thought. "Johnny, you got a wife or steady girl?"

"No, sir."

"Good. You don't need one right now. Too much to do."

By the end of the summer, John is ensconced in readying his first property, Century Service Garage in Cedarhurst, sometimes spending day and night on site sleeping on an Army cot in a back office. Two nights a week he broke away to attend classes: not for credit—he had done that—but for the knowledge. He liked auditing electronics and engineering classes for fun as well as keeping abreast of research and development.

#

My father's invention—the first Universal Backup Light—advanced earlier patterns that had begun in 1921. His was automatic and accessible. In addition to mechanical acumen and personal challenge, his purpose, and therefore design, was prevention, protection, and availability. He attached value to safety and saw it as a feature that should be within reach of all drivers not just the wealthy who could afford a new car with the safety device already installed. Small but critical, his was the first *universal* automatic backup light switch. As he wrote in an application, *"Designed and manufactured my own backup light switch, automatic (patented). Engaged in the manufacture of automotive accessories and electrical devices."*

There had been earlier rudimentary versions of the device, but this one was universal, obtainable, generic to most models, and allowed a singular inexpensive purchase rather than the exclusiveness of a factory-fitted new car accessory. I remember feeling a part of something very important when I assembled little cardboard boxes my father brought home for me. It was a nice gesture but not necessary to the effort. By then he had Harben in Hewlett and a manufacturing factory in Brooklyn filled with several employees dedicated to shipping early orders. Sears, Roebuck and Co., by contract, was poised to distribute.

The name John Frank Huszar might have been carved on the tablet of auto industry history, but his integrity and a broken heart intervened. He had taken two partners: his trusted bookkeeper and a silent investor. And because he cared so much for these two men, he actually created the name of the new company from letters associated with their names. It became the Harben Company in honor of Harold Lenane and Ben(rus). It was typical of my father to give credit to, even promote, others. He wasn't about getting the glory, and his offer of a blended name shows his deep respect for their friendships. Therefore, later when the embezzlement was discovered, it was shocking and painful beyond belief: Harold had stolen much more than money: it was a theft of the soul.

My father would have nothing more to do with the man who would rob from a friend. He simply, sorrowfully, walked away from the broken bond. The patent, the Sears contract, nothing meant anything anymore after such a violation of trust. He had the opportunity to press charges against his employee for the felony crime, but he sought no revenge. He believed his duplicitous former friend and colleague would one day be judged in the only court that truly matters. Riches already being enjoyed by this artist of embezzlement and future royalties that would follow if he continued manufacturing assured Harold Lenane great wealth. But never the pride of success: "For what will it profit a man if he gains the whole world and forfeits his soul?" (Matthew 16:26) (English Standard Version)

The crook did not continue manufacturing: the business was sold and the investor satisfied. With the sale providing him newfound financial security that could last a lifetime, Harold Lenane was free to live well on the genius of another. **The irony is that he moved his family to what may very well have been the temptation that s**oiled the man—a mansion in Hewlet Bay Park. *It was also home to Mr. Lazarus and where my father had already begun scouting for a modest version of a house in the Park. I still remember the day he drove me around the sunken beauty of the Hewlett hamlets, stopping to announce, 'And here is where you will be going to school, Lizzie.'*

"No one ever called me Lizzie, my middle name, except my father. It was his mother's first name, and he wanted to honor her. Apparently my mother prevailed in the name sequence: I always wished she had put the pretty name, Elizabeth, first and Janice second. Because he was so hurt, my father relinquished his partnership prematurely in an emotional decision *without considering future returns, taking nothing but a token—four hundred dollars, I think—as settlement. What mattered more to him was that he too was free to live well, not on the intellectual property of another, and never in the company of deceit, but honorably earned, as he knew no other way.*

Indeed it behooved the wrongdoer to sell and hurry away from the scene. The deceit had been well planned: sell and sever, receive the spoils, hide the records, and do the laundry.

Indicative of the greed was the grand appetite of the nouveau riche man: Harold Lenane's lust led not only to a transfer from his comfortable home on a simple Hempstead street to the lush landscape of the ultra-wealthy enclave, Hewlett Bay Park/Hewlett Harbor, but to a second residence nestled in the beautiful White Mountains of New Hampshire.

The first splurge of the out-of-hiding monies, however, was the purchase of a coveted high-class home with its posh address in the Hewlett wetlands. Secluded, and an almost-closed society, it was home to many Manhattan millionaires, primarily from high finance and the budding television industry. To this day there are affluent commuters with private drivers traveling between the city networks and the luxury of their Long Island xanadu.

#

After a much-needed respite, my father returned to work, but he never again built a business. He never spoke about the tragedy, never complained, never told anyone how it feels to have a dream realized, only to be stolen by a trusted friend. And as he did as a child who triumphed over abandonment, he did in the loneliness of his grief: he counted his blessings. And there are always many, ever so close. They don't have to be big to be beautiful: watching a tiny backyard bird will make you smile, but never a bear. A fragile kitten will snuggle and purr on your lap, and you go soft against your will. No gold, silver, nor diamonds can compare to the sparkle of a long-awaited homecoming. It doesn't take much: just look around and accept God's blessings, from the tiniest to over the top. It's a Johnny remedy for any age. It takes very little: just turn and look upward.

#

My father's memory of his mother was more essence than image. He could remember she was slender and full of fun, the curls in her hair always bouncing when she moved fast, and very beautiful he would add with a smile, aware of course that almost every boy feels that way about his mother. A mother's love is summer sun all year round, warm and nourishing, protecting and providing. When memories are few, and longing still alive, we reach back and try to remember the glow and carefree days of childhood with our mothers that are so precious, and perhaps inspirational, to us now. In those sacred nights when mother and son said their prayers together, she also read Scripture, little lines of wisdom to keep close. The quiet of those moments had a sound, a melody all its own, so soft and pleasing to the ear.

*My son, obey your father's commands, and don't neglect your
mother's teaching. Keep their words always in your heart.
Tie them around your neck. Wherever you walk, their counsel can
lead you. When you sleep, they will protect you. When you wake
up in the morning, they will advise you. For these commands
and this teaching are a lamp to light the way.*
Proverbs 6:20–23
ESV

Now a return to the happy days of Harben, that sweet season of unblemished friendship and common goal that fueled the fires of achievement before evil took its breath away....

John has been learning to delegate responsibility and rely more on his initial employees so that he can devote time to his <u>universal</u> backup light. By the holidays he has opened two new businesses. The demands are so exhausting that he rarely has time to indulge in a favorite pastime: the morning paper with a cup of good coffee. Instead he dashes out of his tiny apartment and begins early duties with coffee and doughnuts hurriedly consumed along the way. So he never saw her picture in the social section of the *New York Herald Tribune*. It was lovely, the words brief: "Mr. and Mrs. Alfred Castle of Inwood, Long Island, announce the engagement of their daughter, Mabel Eleanor, to Russell Gordon, a resident of New Jersey. No date has been set for the wedding at this time." Even if he had leisure time to sit with coffee and read the paper, it's doubtful John would have turned to the social pages. In fact, it's a given.

The relationship between Mr. Lazarus and John has grown far beyond dollars dutifully repaid each quarter. The investor-mentor is delighted with his prodigy. He feels rewarded. Blessed. Good to be back in the game. He would have invited Johnny to his sprawling home by the water more often for the smart and serious, sometimes even humorous hours of enjoyment, except he knows the effort John puts into the businesses and doesn't want to intrude into his quiet time, if any. But occasionally the elder will call and ask him to visit, just frequently enough to share in his achievements and bask in his company. His feelings for John run deep. So much so that he modified his will to include "forgiveness" of John's debt if still existing at his death. But John had satisfied the debt early, without knowledge of the codicil to Mr. Lazarus's will. Only years later by a notice of the reading of the will did John learn of the thoughtful gift his dear friend had prepared. Though never needed, its loving purpose lived on in John's heart.

#

John has learned to relegate and reduce his duties, enabling him to visit Mr. Lazarus more often. It follows an earlier suggestion. The older man comes to life when the younger comes to visit. And if his health is failing, at least his spirit improves. The visits are special to both. Three walls lined with beautifully bound classics, the fourth all glass for a spectacular view of verdant landscape hugging the terrace and a rambling perfect lawn leading down to a spacious gazebo by the pond sets a stage of splendor. It is more, though, than the view and the elegance of the library, or the merit of the man so accomplished and kind: it is profound peace that John experiences when there. Unspoken pleasure. The three Lazarus brothers had emigrated many years ago, and so had John's father and mother. From different countries but to the same shore, they shared in and passed on a legacy of risk, hard work, and love. It begets peaceful thought.

"Tell me about your holidays, Johnny," the elder asks. "You were on my mind: I hoped you weren't alone. I wasn't feeling well so it was a subdued holiday here; even no noise for the New Year."

"You should have called," John says immediately, saddened to think of Mr. Lazarus suffering.

"No, nothing serious. Not to worry. Just some lazy days with my bride." Of course, he means his first and only wife and partner, Mrs. Lazarus, to whom he is devoted. "And, we don't celebrate the same here as you do anyway. Our Hanukkah, both sacred and festive, runs eight sequential nights and days between late November and late December according to the Hebrew calendar. So we're big on candles." He smiles at his guest, wondering if he understood it as humor, while he walks over to the bar and pours each a brandy.

He tries another bit of humor when he hands John the snifter: "But we're sober-thinking for the gift giving," he says, with a smile returned with understanding.

"I did have a nice holiday, Mr. Lazarus," John says, "and I appreciate your sending the baskets of delicacies to each of the shops, and of course, my handsome wristwatch. I admit it was a quiet Christmas, but actually it was just what I needed. Time to recoup, store up energy for another possible opening as you recommended, and to continue working on introducing my backup light."

"I love it! Can you tell how your energy rubs off on me, Johnny? It is an old man's therapy."

"You made it all possible, sir."

He wishes he could do something great for this man, but he needs nothing. He is fulfilled: he is educated, and has accomplished so much. Benrus has become a popular and trusted name here at home and abroad. He has known love. He has had the joy of children in his life. And he has shared his blessings. It is indeed self-actualization. And John hopes to follow, but now he can only vow to pass on the teachings of this good man of wisdom and kindness to someone else along the way. Pay back the debt by extending to another what has been given so graciously to him.

"Mind a little fatherly advice, Johnny?" He liked to call him that rather than simply John.

"No sir, you know I welcome it."

"Branch out a little. Get some balance in your life. Not always so serious. Go to a movie. Have a beer. And work on your managerial skills.

"Now I know you got yourself some degree a few years back. But you need to be street smart too because you know there are some things you can't find in any classroom. Book learning is untested learning. You got to go with those who've been there. You want to hear from the ones who've made it. Done it. And listen good [sic] to their stories."

"Thank you, Mr. Lazarus. Your wisdom and support are immeasurable. A very special gift."

"I know you mean that, Johnny, but that's not what I'm talking about. Seminars are springing up all over: lectures on hiring and firing, motivating employees, grooming for management … things like that, that you don't always learn from pages in a book. Or chatting with another novice. You got to hear it from the ones who do it. I'd like to see you attend some of them. The best speakers are in the city. And there's good camaraderie. Good contacts. Will you take a little time out for one?"

"Absolutely. When do we go?" Johnny will do anything his supporter suggests. Not only because he trusts the man but because he wants to please him in any way he can. Mr. Lazarus is doubly pleased. He hadn't planned on attending with him, and is honored that Johnny's mind works that way.

"Next one that comes along, we'll sign up," Mr. Lazarus says. So now he has a purpose too. His health has lowered his metabolism: but already he's feeling renewed. He will introduce his protégé to the unfamiliar, the Manhattan side of business not yet explored. He is putting finishing touches on his already HVA, high value asset. They try never to minimize the deep respect and rich friendship they share, but distance, health, family attention, business demands, and a new faster paced way of life steadily intervene. And the trauma of thievery masked as loyalty in a pretense of trusted friend, employee, and partner roles has turned John's life upside down. The never expected betrayal has broken his heart and his spirit.

Contact with Mr. Lazarus consequently wanes. The attack on John and his businesses has taken a toll, robbing him even further, by loss of time.... Not exactly legal research, but John devotes himself to seeking a reason— health? debt?—that his friend could turn to such dishonesty. Unrelenting sadness quietly colors John's day and inhibits full concentration. But it is never mentioned, and no legitimate reason for such hateful behavior has ever surfaced.

Cordial telephone calls and an occasional handwritten note replace personal visits to Mr. Lazarus and serve as a reminder to each that their special bond was of love.

CHAPTER XVIII

It's providential: John would never have been sitting at any convention had Mr. Lazarus not suggested their value. This time he is alone, a second venture into the world of lectures chosen for its appealing headline: How to Manage Increasing Demands of the Automotive Industry. It is a two-day event in mid-Manhattan for which he registered in advance, also booking an overnight at the Biltmore. His mentor is sitting this one out. John rides up to the twenty-second floor grand ballroom, now transformed by rows and rows of chairs well packed with look-alike businessmen in tailored pinstripe suits and vests, seemingly to differ only by background colors. The success set, or at least dressed and ready for it. Johnny squeezes his way to a seat in the far corner, opens his notebook, reaches for his pen, and awaits the speech for Session One, "Establishing Leadership Goals."

Minutes later all is quiet, announcements and introductions then made, and applause for the first speaker begins as he approaches the lectern. A few cute opening remarks spark laughter from the audience, and then it happens. That word. The very word Johnny always knew he would recognize immediately if ever he were to hear it. It rings in his ears, pulsing with repetition, as his heart in perfect tune triggers spotted memory....

The man has just said, "In my hometown of Renovo, Pennsylvania..." and John hears nothing beyond Renovo except the drumbeat of his chest.

Not a word of the man's ongoing speech reaches him; everything seems to have stopped. Renovo! That's it. Just a word, but life-giving for one so long deprived. It's real to him now. It's home. He sits still so the rapid heartbeat will slow itself, and the disorientation of shock dissolves into the bliss of answered prayer. He draws deep breaths and then softly exhales, finally feeling back to life: and with that, he leaps up from his chair, gathering the unnecessary papers under his arm and pushing past the pin-stripers in his row, walking fast—wishing to run—down the center aisle, swinging open the double door onto the hallway where the elevator door is already open for an express trip down to the main lobby. And the telephone booths. He wants to call someone, needs to tell someone, herald the news, but in a moment of clarity he realizes there is really no call to make. There is no one to whom it would matter. Except one, maybe. Yes, there is one person that once seemed to really care. Who made a promise....

#

"Mabel?" She knows right away. Though out of breath it is still his voice, the sound of which she has never forgotten. And he rang her with a number he has never forgotten.

"Hello, John. This is a surprise. Are you all right? You sound so, oh I don't know, out of breath or something, overexcited, or in trouble? What's wrong? Hopefully nothing.... You're okay, right? I...."

"Stop a minute," he says. "Yes, I'm okay. I know it's been a long time, Mabel, and I am well acquainted with what you said in your letter. I've respected that. But I do believe in promises. As you do. And maybe I'm just an idealist, but when someone gives me their word, I like to think they mean it, that I can count on it, hold them to it in the same way I expect my promises to matter, to count to the other person."

"John, I don't understand what you're talking about: I made no serious promises, no commitments to you if that's what you mean. I have other obligations now. I never made a covenant with you."

"You don't remember, do you?" he asks. "Sitting across the table from me, our first date, when I told you about my aunt and uncle, and you said together we'd find them…."

"Oh, that." She sounds dismissive.

"But then I told you I didn't even know the name of the town I was born in or where we had lived. Well, I know now, Mabel. I just heard it. A man giving a speech a few minutes ago said it, Renovo … and as soon as I heard the name, I knew that's where I was born. I just thought maybe you'd like to know. And I'm going to drive there in the morning.

"I'm sorry I've been rambling; I shouldn't have called. It's just that I'm so excited I wanted to share my news with someone special. Forgive me for interrupting; I hope you weren't terribly busy, or even worse, in the middle of dinner with others. I should let you get back to whatever you were doing. I apologize."

"How have you been, Johnny? I hope well."

"Fine, yes, fine; just fine," he says.

She hesitates, because she knows this is the moment of truth. Her truth, her moment, not the father's, not the mother's. It belongs to her.

Mabel grows up in this moment. "Johnny, where are you for goodness' sake?"

"Standing at a pay phone in the lobby of the Biltmore Hotel in Manhattan. Haven't you heard the coins? I'm drawing a little crowd here I'm afraid."

"Stay there," she says. "Don't change your mind and leave tonight. I'm catching the next train. Will you meet me at Penn Station?"

He can't answer. Can't speak. Good thing he's in a telephone booth able to hide the tears now streaming down his face, although too full of emotion to really care; the phone is still gripped in his hand as he leans against the narrow glass pane door for stability. He isn't listening, isn't even trying to respond. He just stands there looking at the phone in his hand, her faint voice barely coming through. "Johnny, Johnny are you there? Answer me, John! Oh, never mind. I'm on my way. Just be there."

And she knew he would.

#

It was easy to slip away unnoticed. All it took really was an emergency call to Crowell, one she instinctively understood and joined in for safe hiding. Mabel had no time to explain, but Crowell knew it was a change of heart—no, an admission of heart—and she is delighted for her young friend. For both of them: she loves Johnny too. Mabel quickly packs an old lightweight suitcase she found in the attic, one no one would ever miss. Using white tissue paper, she delicately folds her undergarments and pajamas and two wrinkle-free dresses perfect for riding in a car. With comfortable shoes, soft slippers, and minimal toiletries she is done and hurries across the boulevard to her sister's house for a ride to the station. She trusts Mary with this new secret, and Mary hugs her with great happiness. She never wanted Russell in the family. It is a blessing that the parents always retire to bed early and use a radio to keep the outside world at bay. In the morning they will let Mabel sleep in after last week's busy schedule at Wave Crest. They like to allow her that rest when she comes home exhausted. The father will go to his office. The mother will bake in the morning for the women of the church prayer circle later in the day. Mary, a teller, will be at her post in the Lawrence-Cedarhurst Bank, and Fred at his in the Peninsula Bank. Edith is expecting Arlene Montgomery for lunch after which she will cook ahead for Louie's dinner and prepare an always delicious fresh fruit dessert. No one will miss Mabel today, tomorrow, or the next; perhaps even several more days hidden behind a simple assumption of "on duty." Questions naturally would go to Crowell, well prepared for double talk.

The train slows to its dark entry into underground Manhattan where even at that hour a herd of passengers run for the exit. The same kind gentleman that earlier lifted up Mabel's suitcase now removes it from above and bids her good evening. She wonders if he wonders about her destination. Did her face light up like her heart? She watched him descend the steps and turn to walk away ... and if she were in a bit of a daze from the emotion of the last two hours, watching that man disappear on the platform reminds her she should be doing the same. Johnny will be here. Of that she is sure. In minutes she will see him. He always did stand out in a crowd. She picks up the suitcase and her small pocketbook and moves from the aisle to the wobbly connection of two cars where she stands on the top step for a moment, holding to the precarious railings but not accepting the conductor's hand.

John notices her immediately: she is the quintessence of womanhood and the most beautiful sight of his life. He politely, just-for-a-moment, positions himself in front of the conductor at the bottom of the stairs as love steps down into his arms.

The conductor applauds.

#

Holding hands, they make their way off the platform and up the stairs into a more maddening crowd pushing and shoving and now on this level shouting out for taxicabs. John's car is parked just a few blocks away, and they run to it ahead of the rain just announced by a few droplets. They see little of the mighty Hudson River—so late is their crossing of the George Washington Bridge, but never mind: the only sightseeing that matters this trip is of each other.

Picking up speed on the open road, Johnny asks Mabel if she had dinner before his call, and she had, just as he had had a meal before signing in for the miracle at the Biltmore. Was she tired? Should he stop? No, she was too happy to be tired, she said. They sped along the popular east west highway knowing there would be adequate shelter for them when they were ready.

"Oh, Mabel, this is unbelievable: that you're really here beside me. I just love you so."

"And I love you, Johnny." That she knows beyond any doubt now. And isn't that what Dada had actually asked her to do? Find out once and for all? She will remind him of that during the heated discussion that is sure to take place.

Johnny doesn't expect an apology, but Mabel needs to explain. "Part of me wanted you to, I don't know, contact me some way even though I said not to in my letter." She begins to unravel the mystery of her heart. "It wasn't that my father was forbidding me to see you. To the contrary, he was suggesting that I see you but see Russell as well. I just couldn't do that to you, Johnny. It didn't seem fair. I wanted to make the right decision, but that takes time, and somehow I just fell, as if powerless to stop, into a spinning web, a cycle of events that led me in a different direction. I don't know, it was like a withdrawal from you not my own, incrementally choreographed from behind. I don't like to think that, but.... Anyway, I'm to blame too: I rationalized in self-talk: 'If you really cared, you'd have followed up on me: driven by my family's home, attempted to reach me by phone, a note or card, even a call to Crowell. And, when you didn't do any of that, it reinforced my decision, or better said acceptance, that I was born to be with Russell. But I actually never made a set-in-stone decision, except to go back to work at WC and to postpone the reception "deposits" for definite dates to the ire of the Gordons. I think they could see what I could not—that delay was really decision.

"That's essentially what was happening to me. I don't know. I just think that all along, even after my curt letter, I've been secretly hoping that you'd come and forcefully whisk me away." She looked over at him for a reply though the car was dark and she knew he was focused on the road. But he did speak, with eyes straight ahead.

"In a way, it's looking like God's way: this has turned out perfectly, by design, Mabe. I wouldn't have wanted you if still you were confused or vulnerable to further coercion and especially not if it were my sad face tugging at your soft heart that led you back to me. No, it was important that you come to me of your own volition: freely, your choice, from the depth of your soul. It wouldn't have worked any other way. And though your return to me was accelerated by my call, it was the honesty of your love that brought you back."

She knew he was right. He was such a smart man. There was so much about him she loved. How could she have ever been persuaded to reconsider Russell after knowing Johnny?

"I never really considered you would be engaged," John says. "I suspected it in a way, but couldn't believe in its possibility. I felt you knew better. I'm sorry for—what's his name? Okay, Russell Gordon. Well, to your Mr. Gordon I can only say, 'Looks like the best man won.'"

#

It wasn't many miles before their day to remember rolled over to the next in a timely signal for rest. The fever pitch of their evening has been an assault on each by a powerful emotional charge: hurried hours to unplanned destinations and 'an intensity of together' so deep that they have no other appetite. But they do crave sleep and in the slow-lifting darkness of a new day morning drive to the first motel with lights still at their window.

It will not be a romantic respite. Mabel deserves much better. They both do: each has been saving for marriage, so tonight is just a pause by demand, for sleep. Like a long nap, but not together: John expects to wait for the preordained day of their union. He is very respectful of his only love. And for the next days they travel in a pattern of deliberateness toward finding Renovo. It begins with a good breakfast, light lunch, healthy early dinner, and a shared chocolate dessert. The rest of the evening belongs to them. Except the long days of driving and less-than-perfect accommodations rule: they surrender to their exhaustion. After driving on highways and across a part of the plain, through established villages, the zigzag trek into the wilderness that is the center of Pennsylvania is challenging. Tomorrow they'll begin to see the majesty of mountains. John has missed them: their peaks proud members of a portrait sky and their valleys birthing rivers for life-giving freshwater fish, and game. But along with the beauty he remembers what he does not: and forgotten feels eerie. Many years have passed: he might not find what he's been looking for. However, he found Mabel again because of this, and that is the real gift. They are within reach. They probably could press on after dinner and arrive late in the night, but that would not serve them well. They'd be tired in the morning, maybe sleep late and miss valuable office hours of searching historical records and current city files for local leads to John's aunts and uncle. Also, John would like to dine in a nice restaurant with his beloved without the pressure of getting back on the road. They could indulge in a decadent dessert, maybe take a walk around a little village, and just enjoy a quiet evening before tomorrow's special event of entering Renovo.

"So that's what we'll do then, stay overnight here," John says. He turns the car around to look for the country lodge Mabel thinks she saw at the outskirts of town.

"It was a little bit back from the road," she says. "Maybe quarter of a mile; I don't know, but it looked nice."

Not too long after, in fact close to her calculation, Mabel sees it: "Oh, yes, that's it. Right over there," she points. "And isn't it lovely?"

"I don't know that I'd call it lovely; maybe 'quaint.' Seems reminiscent of an English inn. And I'm sure that inside it's, well, lovely."

"Stop grinning," Mabel says, smiling herself at the dig. As he pulls into the property, she suggests he park over by the other cars, but he doesn't. He drives up to the front entrance, idles the car, gets out and goes around to help her down from the running board.

"You go on in; I'll be right back," he says, opening the door for her with a wave to the innkeeper as a signal of his return. If there's a vacancy, he'll go back for the suitcases. Good thing he had one packed for that night at the Biltmore.

Mabel watches John walk back from the car. Still not sure of a vacancy, only a dinner, he carries nothing except a happy heart. And it shows in his step. The owner-innkeeper invited them to sit by the fireplace, burning no doubt to create Old English ambience. There is a multicolor braided rug in front of fenced flames, but no golden retriever resting there, though requisite in popular pubs. A dartboard on the short wall to the left was twin to the one on the right, and a variety of wines and liquor on shelves behind a high dark wood bar defined it for sure. True pub.

Yes, of course, they have a vacancy: last one. Yes, the dining room is still open. Yes, they are delighted to have Mr. and Mrs. Huszar as guests for the night.

John was surprised by the assumption, but why go into a personal conversation that might then lead to their being asked to find other lodging? He's not sure they offer single rooms, but by asking he would invite curiosity and a possible path to outside. Mabel likes it so well here he doesn't want to risk the possibility of disappointment. The man was very nearly correct, though, anyway. They will wait joyously for their date to become Mr. and Mrs. John Huszar in their home church as soon as possible. Mabel watches as John registers, feeling giddy all of a sudden after hearing Mrs. Huszar being called. She simply does not invite attention to the sweet mistake and follows the innkeeper down the hall to open the door. John is right behind and quickly enters using a handshake and a 'thank you' smile to quickly turn the man around and ease him toward the open door. And just to be sure, after closing it, Johnny presses his back fully against the door, standing there to take a mental picture of the beauty before him. Of course they embrace: their kisses unstoppable in dreamlike passion. But they must pull apart and hurry to dinner: there are two sittings, and this is the second. As they walk down the hall, John realizes he has not asked Mabel how she feels in regard to the owner's mistake: does she want to leave after dinner, or should he inquire about single rooms? Then again, he knows her: she would want to be near each other, but in a room with single beds. Yes, they think alike. It needn't be discussed. They believe in God's purpose for denying desire and waiting for the sacrament of marriage before sharing in the beauty of the unspoken language of love.

And John can easily withstand the wait for the gift of marriage that is ahead: he's been well trained in the school of delay. God provides in so many ways: the practical as well as spiritual. And John turns to the practical right now.

"Do you think you should call your family, Mabel? They'll be worried about you. Reveal as much or as little as you need at this time. Say whatever you feel is right."

"No, that's okay. Crowell is covering. I think it's best not to have any communication until we're all together," she says. "My parents will be thinking I'm on double duty for several days yet. They don't often call me there. It'll work; don't worry about it. I have put it aside to concentrate on us.

"Actually Russell is more of a concern," she adds. "If he calls Wave Crest and someone other than Crowell, without script, answers, it could get messy. He would follow with a call to my parents, most likely, and cause a great deal of fear.

"Maybe I should initiate a quick call to him, John, and tell him something has come up that I must tend to out of town, and that I will contact him as soon as possible because it's important. I know he will sense the personal gravity. I can't lie: everything I just said is indeed a fact. Yes, I shall call him. Later. Tomorrow when he's in his office."

"Oh, my goodness, how delicious the aroma," Mabel says as they enter the forest green and mahogany dining room with just the right soft lighting for English elegance. "Thank you, Johnny, for bringing me here," she says.

"You're welcome," he says, thinking he should be thanking her. This is real time, and the blessing is tangible.

CHAPTER XIX

"There it is! Just like the man at the pump said: look for the fork in the road," Mabel says. John slows down, veers to the right, and drives the six miles in silence. Not very far down the road is a small handmade arrow hammered on a tree, pointing to Renovo. Surely the city deserves a better introduction than that, if only for its prolific railroad yards. Mabel is excited getting so close to the gold, but respects the silence Johnny needs as he enters his past. It has the look of a city, small of course, but different from the rural valley hamlet John had imagined it to be. He would learn it had been incorporated back in 1866, at a time when the economy was dependent on lumbering. And when the trees of the first growth forest were brought to bare with nothing more to give, the loggers lost their livelihood. Then the trains came.

They were on the fast track, and Renovo grew alongside the success of the rail industry and its related businesses. The mighty Pennsylvania & Erie Railroad, a kind of patriarch overseeing hundreds of families arriving for work in the railroad yards, had designed an urban grid for the rapid growth of Renovo. The workers could purchase little plots of land for side-by-side homes, or even closer, participate in popular row houses. All their necessities were easily available in the Pennsylvania Railroad Shops right there within the construction yards. John is in a world of his own right now, and in a way it's familiar. He's able to remember a little bit from the tableau coming to life before him. But everything seems smaller than before. There is a stand-alone cement square-as-a-box building memorable for its facade of many colors across from the creamery that appears to have shrunk. Of course, everything looms larger in childhood. And he doesn't know yet of the big flood that almost took the town away. It rearranged lives and property, even attitude. Living by the river requires respect for its power. The unexpected violence taught a good lesson to the community and inspired protective measures, ongoing as society matures into a world of modern convenience.

Before they begin their inquiries, John simply has to drive around the streets for a couple of minutes: "This is bringing back so much, Mabel. Over there," he points, "that's where I know I walked with my mother and aunts; and I remember I rode a bike with Papa steadying my seat as I learned to balance on a tiny two-wheeler."

He slides into a parking space near the playground recognizable for its dizzying round-about and low-to-the-ground cement pond with a curb, and the signs that permit only pocket-size boats. A memory of windy days guiding the white sails of his little boat comes into focus.

"Oh my goodness, I can almost see it: blue, of course, my favorite color."

Mabel smiles at the discovery but is not yet quite up to date with his thoughts. They walk from the car, hand in hand, and stand a few minutes watching the little children launching their boats, a sweet remembrance of yesteryear.

They head for the courthouse just a block away and are greeted graciously. As they stand side by side at the counter, they hear bleak news: "I'm sorry, there are no records here," the clerk says. "Not since the big flood in '36. Everything was destroyed, or almost everything anyway, when the west branch of the Susquehanna overflowed and just about wiped our little town away. Those waters even reached the railroad wall over on fourteenth. I'm telling you it was some disaster. Deep snows melting high in the mountains is what caused it. We're just lucky it hasn't happened again.

"What could be saved of our public records they keep at the county seat over at Lock Haven now. That's where you'll want to go. And just to be sure, we are Clinton County."

"Thank you, sir. But I'd like to visit in your little town before leaving it. Could you direct me to the Catholic Church, or a town historian, one of the older doctors maybe? You see, I'm trying to find out something about my family. I was born here." Johnny notices how nice it is to be able to say that, how easily it rolls out.

"Well, in that case, you really want to see old Doc Valeo. He knows this town better than any other person, from his birthing most of us. But come to think of it, he's off visiting his daughter out of state somewhere right now. The priest over at St. Joe's: he's too young; wouldn't remember any of our generation. Only been serving this parish a year or so. Tell you what, go on over and see the minister of our Community Church. Wendell does the preaching; him [sic] and Ann, they've been around here for years. Maybe they can help you," the man says, drawing a little map with their address.

"I hope so," John says. "And I really appreciate your time. Thank you. Good bye." Johnny grabs Mabel's hand, and they start to leave, almost missing the chorus of "Good luck," called out from those at the counter.

"So that's what I would recommend, wouldn't you, Wendell?" The soft-speaking, grey-haired lady is serving tea to her guests. Although John had knocked on the door without warning, Ann was delighted to have their company. Maybe John and Mabel would like to visit their church and hear a sermon by her husband if they're still in town on Sunday, she's thinking. But Ann defers to Wendell in anything so bold as "bringing in the sheaves."

"Yes, of course I agree," Wendell says. "Charlie Whitman over at Faraday has been the watchman of our town, dare I say, from its inception. He would have known your father, I believe: been around for ages, never missed a thing. We don't have an official position, but if we did, town historian would surely be his title."

John and Mabel, eager to be on their way but not wanting to be rude, accept the homemade brownies and a second cup of tea. Then the lovely Mrs. Carlson shows them to the door, hugs each, and wishes them success. Wendell, too arthritic to leave his chair—"there are good days and bad days"—has already blessed the young couple. She closes the door.

John's roadster shines its way through little streets of Old-World charm, not actually picturesque but spirit-filled with gratitude and optimism and cinnamon. A hint of Hungarian cuisine travels as musk in the open convertible, deliciously deciding for them that only a true ethnic dinner will do tonight. They look left to right, again and again, as they scan the streets marveling at the obvious pride of ownership—the quintessential white lace curtain at every front window just above the flower box—and trying to absorb as much valley life as possible. They feel a real sense of stepping back in time: his mother's time. Lizzie Illar. Lost too soon. And if her death were, as some suggested, due to the horrors of the flu pandemic of 1918, she may not even have had a proper burial: hundreds of bodies not embalmed were piled up on Renovo's streets, unless buried in one of the mass graves filled with plywood caskets shipped in to help the hard-hit city. But Lizzie did have proper attention: John remembers a coffin by the window and darkly dressed mourners sitting with heads bowed. He couldn't know about any plans for the following days, however: his father took him away that night. The town was once a busy place, springing up as a result of the railroad junction.

Today, as this is written, the little town of only sixteen blocks is again quiet after early boom years that were followed by decline and then a burst of patriotic activity, especially in the railroad yards during World War I and the Second World War. Although FDR formally announced our neutrality in October 1937, 'The Yards' at Renovo turned from trains to tanks and aircraft equipment, armed with experience having built war materials to aid Britain, the Soviet Union, and China, along with increasing our own readiness for possible Pacific threats. But for John and Mabel their visit in 1939 was sweetly romantic: the attack on Pearl Harbor that would launch us into binary war and the vital role that Renovo would play were far from their imagination. They were in love: that's what they thought about. In fact, most people were living without fear at that time.

But it was very different over at the Yards and down at Lock Haven where Piper Cubs were being produced for the military in rapid succession. The yards and the airplane factory were essential to providing aircraft, trucks and jeeps, and other machinery related to war. It would be a nonstop effort for years, with swing shifts sharing the rhythm of nuts and bolts on metal in an orchestra of cymbals and high C's ringing in repetitive duty around the clock, on orders from the government. They were critical jobs in a world about to be set on fire.

Later when war ceased—the European theatre first in May 1945, the Pacific in surrender after our atomic bombs turned Hiroshima and Nagasaki, and their many people, into ashes—the relief was imperfect. The ultimate high price of so many lives lost by brave men and women fighting far from home tarnished the glow of American triumph. Many heroes never returned. Of those who did many were scarred for life by amputation or debilitating injuries, or by violent dark dreams of guilt for their own survival. And others, having not served due to a disabling issue, parental status, or age, suffered also, from guilt for not being there. But together they shared a common bond we still honor today: willingness and readiness to risk their lives for the gift of freedom for others.

#

Renovo was destined to become the little town that was. Even though so prominent in the production of vital equipment for the military troops, when the war ended so did the need, causing most of the 400 workers to move on in order to provide for their families in emerging competition. Renovo succumbed to modernization: a new seaway, a never-before Interstate Highway, and ever-increasing automobile ownership replaced the era of locomotives. And the essential Pennsylvania railroad shops once thriving in the Renovo Yards fell victim to consolidation: the closest shopping area on the new map too far from home. The shops had provided local employment and sustenance for the city and its mountainside neighbors for so many years that the loss was heartbreaking and impossible to reverse. But still the native generational families remain, and retirees continue to draw near the surrounding raw beauty of nature and its resident game. The splendor of alpine streams and waterfalls, wild flowers, clean and clear air; trout fishing, hunting, and silent skies that sparkle with stars cannot be taken away. Nor can the elk that roam and rule so near to heaven.

John stops the car at the last paved street. No need to get out: the top is down, allowing for a picture-perfect view and the crisp mountain air he misses. It is distinctly different from sea level life. And he and Mabel, without words, savor it. The streets and storefronts look familiar.

"I wonder, did my mother shop here in town for groceries, or did she rely mostly on local farm produce and game? Certainly the deer and elk, turkey and wild pork so nearby were our protein, as were the riches of the river. The pristine water, cold and clear, was vital to our health; indeed our very survival. She would have graced the drug store occasionally, although I don't remember ever going there with her. Hopefully, someone in town will. Let's go over later for an ice cream at the fountain. I sort of know that they have one: I sense it, maybe feel it in memory and picture it in my mind. I just wonder if someone sitting there today will remember my mother or father," John says.

For Mabel the thoughts are different: not so much reflection, not so much a need to know. She is getting acquainted with her new role in life as helper, soul mate, and future wife. Yes, she will be there for her beloved, by his side, for the rest of her life. They drive cross town where Johnny stops the car near the bottom of the hill. There it is, the old Faraday house Wendell spoke of, standing guard over the village from atop its highest hill, overlooking the Susquehanna, the railroad, and the lives of its people. It's where Charlie Whitman grew up—his mother had been a Faraday and bequeathed the homestead to her son, expecting her daughter to marry well—and where he raised his own family. There were many generations of the Faraday line so the name of the house stuck. And its reputation for folklore spread.

John and Mabel walk hand in hand parallel to the tracks along the base of the hill, as Johnny and Papa had done so many years before. It would be a miracle level discovery to find a relic at their feet or for a hint of frozen exposure with snow art. Just walking where they walked, Johnny and Papa, matters somehow. And Johnny is getting closer to his truth. They begin their diagonal climb to the dark grey weathered-wood house alone on the hill. There are two levels and an attic to the home that appears rather precarious on its perch.

A man of many years greets them warmly. He'd already heard about the 'young couple just arrived, looking for the town crier.' "Come in, please, and join me in the parlor. What is it that I can do for you?"

With Mabel at his side and introductions over, John tells a condensed version of his life story: "Loss of mother; taken away by father; left in a flat at amusement park; three-plus years living mostly alone; then the orphanage. That pretty much says it all. What I'm most interested in, Mr. Whitman, is if you knew my parents, Frank and Lizzie Huszar?"

"Well, son, yeah… I did know your pa. Good man, smarter than all of us put together around here; had a heavy accent, though, and it weren't [sic] ours. We might live in the valley, but we're mountain climbing hunters here, still talking like when long ago the Scotch and English migrated over the Appalachian divide, bringing their accents with them. Mixed in with our twang, this is what we got: genuine mountain talk. But not your father: he kept speaking Hungarian style that was used back home in his section of Austria. I know that 'cause I asked, and he was nice to explain it to me.

"He was a builder of railroad cars down at the big yards for sure. And inventor, too. Had a couple of things to his credit I know. So then he gives up the railroad cars to work on his own inventions. That little warning signal they got on the tracks now—that was one of his ideas, I'm thinking."

"Wow," was all John could say. He was remembering the time in the Coney Island flat when Papa sketched two of his father's own invention ideas for him and explained their parts as he went along.

After the pause, John compliments Mr. Whitman: "Sir, you have more than a good memory—you're a walking journal. I am so thankful to have met you. It is an honor for both Mabel and me."

"I'm trying to think," Mr. Whitman says, rubbing his chin, digging deep into memory. "I know something happened around the time he quit the yards ... um, what was it?... Oh, yes, that's right: his young wife died, and he kind of fell apart I think. Can I get you kids anything?"

John was hanging on every word and didn't dare let the man get distracted. "No, no, we're fine, thank you sir. Please go on."

"Sad about the wife," the raconteur continues without connecting that she was John's mother. "Oh, she was a real pretty one; I remember that. Her and the sisters...."

"Great! You knew my aunts too?" The ebullition startled the man and Mabel.

"Sure. I had a good eye for the ladies. Always did. And I see that you do too." He looked over at Mabel admiringly as he spoke. "But it was always innocent: appreciating God's artwork. 'Cause I had the very best: a beautiful princess of a wife for many years. There was only one woman for me, ever. I already can tell you're a good man, John, walking the right path to keeping a happy marriage, like I did.

"That's my hope for you and the missus.

"Thinking back like we're doing, I'm wishing now that I had a news clip or something up in the attic about the yards where your father worked. Or a photograph of the three sisters; I just didn't know them real good [sic]. Sorry to say, I forget their names."

"My mother's name was Lizzie."

The sadness in that simple statement was evident. It evoked silence. John broke the spell. "So then did you know my uncle, too?"

"There was a brother? Oh, yeah, I guess that's right. Of course it is, if you said so. He wasn't around much though; I never really knew him. I'm thinking maybe—but I'm not sure—he mighta [sic] been in vaudeville or something like that."

"A magician," John says. "He traveled around the state and probably in others too, 'cause it was a rare treat to see him. I remember pestering him to take me along, but of course I was much too young for that."

John sees the interview is beginning to tire the elderly man, so he begins to draw it to a close. "Is there anything else you can tell me about my mother?"

"Don't think so," Mr. Whitman says. "Well, they were good Catholics, going to church a lot. I only went on high holy days. The wife, she wasn't Catholic. And sorry to say, I weren't [sic] a good one. 'Forgive me Father.'

"Your mother was pretty, like I already said. I remember 'cause she was nice besides: you could tell there was sweetness there. Always had a smile for you but stuck close to Frank—that's when mostly I saw her: lovebirds, her [sic] and Frank walking around town, looking real proud with their young one. But being frail and all, she ended up real sick. Some of the towns' folk said she had the consumption, and that's why she died. But I think maybe she was one of the thousands of people caught up in that killer pandemic that hit Renovo so hard: hardest in the state some say. But Philadelphia got real hurt too. It woulda [sic] been late fall, 1918." At that, Mr. Whitman stood up from his rocker and put his hand over his heart, bowing in reverence, adding: "Such a pity. God bless their souls."

John agreeing, "Yes sir." Mabel silent. And then a last question: the most important one. "My aunt, the young one, do you think there's any chance she could still be here in town? Or living nearby where I could visit her?"

The old man started to laugh. "You think I'd really be sitting up here all alone if she was? My Lydia made me promise to find a companion after she died. But I haven't fancied anyone to keep company with: I'd rather read and garden, even fix my food, alone. Now, if that youngest sister had stayed living here in town, I might have invited her into friendship. She seemed sweet too. Nice family.

"But they all went together—to where, no one knows. You see, I failed in my duty as volunteer local news gatherer by not knowing that Frank stayed gone, and then that the family just up and left. They couldn't be blamed for wanting to find different scenery: they lost a sister, then brother in-law, and the boy. The empty house was too sad for them, I guess. I shoulda [sic] sensed they might move away from it somehow. I shoulda [sic] been driving by their place, watching them more in my position of watchman," he says with his own sarcastic emphasis on the unofficial title.

"Oh, no, please don't think that way, Mr. Whitman. They deliberately avoided notice of their departure so that they could be private and grieve together in their own way. You couldn't have stopped them; I'm sure of that. You have nothing to regret.

"It was such a pleasure to meet you, sir. I thank you for allowing Mabel and me to come into your home and for taking the time to tell me all you knew about my family. It has meant so very much to me: more than you can know." John stood up as did the gentleman, and they shook hands. Mabel gave Mr. Whitman a hug. It was time to leave.

Mr. Whitman followed right behind them to the front door, still struggling to bring back details of days so long ago. He'd been an old man even then. It wasn't easy to get a memory back into focus. "Wait a minute, son." And John turns around to him. "Now I'm not positive, you hear, but it seems to me that I heard something about the sisters going off to Ohio. Yeah, that was it. They just packed up and moved away, probably with the brother. He would have had a car for his kind of work.

"To Ohio. Or was it Iowa? Well, one of them. Yes, I'm sure. It was definitely one of them."

John smiles, gives him a hug this time. and says, "Well, thank you again, sir. That helps."

Then he and Mabel leave. Mr. Whitman doesn't want John to go. Those questions are bringing clarity to a time and place not usually up front in his mind. "No, don't go yet, John," he calls out, sounding more urgent than before. "I know the last time I saw your pa; sure thing. I know it now. It was of a morning."

And John hears him. And in the cold of that day, the chills of those words quickly turn him around. He reaches for Mabel, and they go back inside the house. They don't speak: just listen.

"Real early it was. I thought nobody else was awake yet, but there he was down there walking right where you two just been coming from. Looked like Frank Huszar to me, walking alongside the tracks, heading to the station, little boy tagging along trying to hold onto his hand until getting picked up and carried rest of the way; that's what I saw that day. It mighta [sic] been raining. Musta [sic] been: I couldn't see too good [sic]. But, yeah, they were walking fast, well Frank was, that morning like hurrying for the train: heading out, holding a bundle under one arm, the boy under the other, low to his hip, like they're leaving town quick [sic], before it wakes up.

"Oh! Oh, dear me…!" He puts his hand over his mouth and his eyes open wide: "Oh, oh, of course, yes, of course," Whitman says. "You must be that little fella in Frank's arms; you are that little boy from that day, of course, aren't ya [sic]?"

Mabel squeezes John's hand. And speaks for him. Tears in her eyes, too. "Yes, Mr. Whitman, he is."

Chapter XX

The sun is setting, afternoon almost over, and with insufficient time to reach Lock Haven before office hours end, John and Mabel are happy to remain in Renovo overnight. They drive back into town to pay a visit to the pharmacy.

The car and the couple are making news. They find it endearing that so many people are waving to them, and they try to return the gesture of welcome in the same way. A few minutes later, after slipping away and into the drug store's hi-back brown leather booth hoping to avoid the curious crowds, they are visited by an out-of-breath Ann Carlson.

"Good, I was afraid maybe you weren't going to sit down and stay long enough for me to catch up to you. Any luck with Mr. Whitman?"

"Yes, it was a pleasant visit, and please sit down," John says. "He remembered my father and a little bit about my mother and her siblings. Thanks again for leading us to him, Mrs. Carlson."

"Ann, please; I'm not formal." She wiggles in beside Mabel. "I'm just glad I could help. And by the way, since it's getting so late, Wendell and I thought maybe you two would come back and join us for dinner. Nothing fancy, but we'd love to have you."

John and Mabel look at each other across the table with smiles of acceptance. Never mind their plan for the ethnic meal. They can always pick up Hungarian-Austrian pastry on the way out of Renovo. "We would enjoy it very much," they say in a duet, though apart. John adds, "Thank you for the invite. What can we do to help you, Ann?"

"We'll think of something when you arrive. Right now, enjoy a treat from the fountain. And ask to speak to the pharmacist, Mr. Hayes, Tim. His father, though quite ill now, might be able to shed some light on your family tree if he is strong enough to accept visitors or take calls. And we'll see you soon, whenever you're ready."

"Do you want to wait a few minutes and let us drive you?" John asks.

"No, thanks; I love a brisk walk."

Two egg creams and a brief conversation later, John and Mabel exit, thankful the crowds have dispersed. "Are you going to call Tim's father?" she asks.

"No, sweetheart, I can't intrude on someone so ill. Even if I knew he had personal stories about my parents, I hope I would surrender the opportunity to privacy at such a solemn time. The son was kind in stepping away from filling prescriptions to speak with us. He seemed nervously protective of his father. I would think even a phone call to the elder is out of bounds now. I understand well the desperate need to preserve a fragile father's ebbing days."

Guests are not allowed in Ann's kitchen: they are royalty while in the Carlson home, an empty nest for too long. The homemade dinner is scrumptious, a real gift after roadside fare. It is an evening of easy laughter, history of the town and its heroes, and a touch of theology. A little persuasion too: the hosts won't hear of John and Mabel going off to a hotel. They insist that they remain for a good night's sleep and an early start right after breakfast. In a soft voice, Ann drives a hard bargain: "We love to have people here. We miss our Billy and his family living so far away in Baltimore. Truly, it would be a good thing. Please don't deny us this pleasure. Billy's room and a bathroom are upstairs: we finished the attic many years ago, and I think you'll find everything you need, John. And Mabel, you have the guest room downstairs, also with a private bath. It too is ready and waiting. So, we're all settled I hope," Ann says. "I will not accept no."

"Nor will I," echoes Wendell.

John brings in their suitcases. "We're blessed this night with new friends and a town we will keep close to our hearts, even from afar," he says as each leaves the front room to retire. Mabel will be lonely without Johnny. But Ann, curious though quiet about the absence of a wedding band, has responded appropriately. She'll wonder, perhaps, but never question the mystery of a missing ring. The bond is obvious; their love deeply authentic; their glow a reflection of God smiling down on his perfectly planned reunion. In fact, both Johnny and Mabel believe the man from Renovo was destined to speak of his hometown early in the program to allow John the time to follow the dots back to Mabel, to Renovo, to everlasting love. God is love. And apparently He delights in matchmaking, although in this case He needed only to mend. What began in a kitchen, slow cooked for several years, and reheated by the beauty of an introduction on a dance floor has come to fruition … and the journey does no stop here.

#

If Lock Haven were not southeast of Renovo with only a half-hour drive off course, John would postpone the courthouse visit for another time. He is concerned about Mabel's family and a little anxious about his businesses too. But an aroma of brewing coffee the next morning brings him downstairs and away from worry, ready to enjoy, leisurely, the country breakfast of eggs and bacon and sausage, biscuits and berries, grits or oatmeal, and fresh orange juice all nicely presented on the dining room buffet. Mabel, still sleepy, comes in at just the right time to carry the last trays from the kitchen, though banned for reentering the room. Cleanup is not for Carlson guests.

Not long after the hearty meal and farewell hugs and the promise to keep in touch, Mabel and Johnny take a last look at Renovo. They park in front of the bakery that soon they shall enter for Austrian strudel, a later dessert, and a gift box of varied miniatures to hand deliver to their impeccable hosts.

"If you'll have a seat, Mr. Huszar, I will see if someone can locate those records for you. You say you believe they are in the files that were retrieved from Renovo after the flood, so we should have them here in Lock Haven. I'll see to it right now; just a moment please." The wait is short, the answer disappointing.

"No, sir, I'm sorry but the records from Renovo during that recovery period have been sent down to Harrisburg, the capital city of our Commonwealth."

"How far is that?" John asks.

"Two hours southeast when weather's good," the employee says.

He calculates the two hours to Harrisburg and another 3.5 hours minimum to New York City, then slow traffic crossing to lower Manhattan with another half hour at least to navigate over to Inwood. This is a conservative total of six and a half hours not including meals; then there are personal stops to consider and the unknown of city traffic. And a long tiring day on the road would make driving into the night unappealing and dangerous. But John doesn't like the idea of losing a day: there must be questions by now. He wants to leave Lock Haven and head home. Mabel wants to continue: she feels they're too close to turn away from real answers.

"We must go on to Harrisburg, Johnny. I simply cannot let you abandon the effort now."

"I'm not abandoning anything, just delaying the last part of the project. It's important to me to get you back home. You can't be absent this long from family without inviting serious concern. And I do have my businesses to look after, too. I can't leave things unattended for too many days. No, we have to save Harrisburg for later."

"No, we don't," Mabel says with conviction. "You know full well that if I were not with you, you'd follow this lead. You are too concerned about my parents and their reaction to our trip. I do not want them to interfere with what you've come to Pennsylvania to do … it is right for you to follow through with this important mission."

John wasn't convinced. "Look, sweetheart, we've accomplished a lot. I know now where to go for next time. But today it's important that I get you back to your work and family. You know they have to be worried by now. I really need to take you home."

"No, Johnny, you don't. Your supervisors can handle things until you return. I'll take care of the parental issue. I know you would go on with your search if you came alone, so I absolutely refuse to hinder it."

She wins. They head south. Harrisburg city limits. Harrisburg city hall. Another clerk, another corridor, and another wait. This time, though, when the woman returns, her words sound like song: "Here you are, Mr. Huszar. There will be no charge for this." He accepts the envelope, staring a moment at its reality so that when he utters 'thank you' as he looks up, the woman has vanished.

Surprisingly, there are several flaws on the certificate of birth: at line number two, the surname is spelled as Hazzar and on line number nine as Huzzar, neither being Huszar, the name with the 's' sound as little Johnny would have first heard. These misspellings are permanent, scars left by a woman's hand that carelessly created a three-way error with flamboyant cursive. She had swirled the pen generously in her duty to enter personal family information on the certificate, ignoring the accuracy official documents demand, in lieu of compliments for pretty penmanship. They were serious errors in three different ways on one page: two were misspellings, the third not spelled at all. She avoided the most common way to spell a most common surname: 'Huszar.' Had she proofed her work, she might have seen the mistakes: inconsistency of two misspelled surnames should have alerted her to check further. She would have learned that Huszar is an extremely popular name in Hungarian/Austrian cultures, and that with so many thousands of people spelling it the way she did not, she needed to correct her error and do the right thing for the exactness expected in official lifelong identification documents. But she did not. And because she lacked initiative and was sloppy in her work, she aroused an unnecessary uncertainty with three options for the surname: her two incorrectly spelled and the one she should have correctly entered. Her carelessness questioned the genesis of our family name. Thankfully, the Brooklyn Children's Aid Society in their intake process relied on the most common Ellis Island spelling, i.e. Huszar, and gave it to Johnny.

He had been, of course, forced to leave his home at age five, fluent in the prevailing English language spoken in the house and familiar with little phrases of Hungarian life that would later slip from memory. Except his name—he would always know that. By his own teaching, he wants to learn to read words like he did with Mama's music. That's when he began to turn old newspapers, magazines, even comics if lucky, into tools for practice. He liked to put letters together. He liked to do what Mama taught.

On an Ellis Island website long after my father's death, our surname as we always spelled it, Huszar, scrolled unendingly until I stopped at page fifty. Seems Huszar is the Smith of Hungary.

They walk over to a window for better sun and huddle together as if reading the morning reviews of a Broadway play. John, holding the paper in his hand, is amazed at its power and potential. It ends years of longing and offers proven birthright and heritage he shall be proud to share with his bride. He focuses on the right side of the precious birth document where truth is told: he learns Lizzie's answers about herself, and by holding the certificate in his hand she becomes almost real for those moments. He reads aloud to Mabel, introducing her to his mother:

"On the day of delivery her age at last birthday was twenty-nine; her birthplace, Austria; occupation, housewife; and one born alive child."

The most blatant of the pen lady's careless misspellings is the surname at the top of the page, line number two, where a proud and identifying full name of a newly born infant is presented to the world. As we already know, in her hurried attitude she recorded—indelibly—the baby's surname as Hazzar instead of Huszar. And she spelled the father's surname wrong, too; but not the same 'wrong' as what she used for the baby. At line number nine, her error has the father's surname as Huzzar. What is curious is the absence of the name Frank on line number nine. There should have been room enough on the line for another word, but it only reads John Huzzar [sic] when John Frank Huszar is the father's true name. The middle name should have been there, right in the center, following the generational legacy of the full family name. Johnny had always heard the name Frank used for his father in the background of his young years while Papa was a favorite moniker for the children. Mr. Whitman referred many times to Frank in the reveries he shared with John and Mabel. Unquestionably, the man, the papa, had always been known as Frank: at home in Renovo, and later when he was lost in New York.

"Everybody who Papa knew personally, and those who knew him by reputation, knew only Frank Huszar, builder of railroad cars and creator of super smart inventions. I am sure my father was born John Frank Huszar, but he used his middle name instead as many of us do. I remember him as a man of sounds: joyous heavy clapping, loud singing, loud laughter, then spoiled by loud arguments with my aunts calling out 'Frank' in angry shrill voices. Yes, it's coming back.

"I was named John Frank Huszar in honor of my father. Our full names are the same, but I was never called Frank. Personally, I don't think my mother was keen on the name. But I'm glad she allowed it for posterity."

It just never made it into the Father box number nine.

For the record, the father was twenty-two at his last birthday; his occupation, well that's another error.... They ask for it at line number fourteen, part of a three-line Occupation box. But the woman with the pen used only one line, swirling just two words in answer: car builder. She forfeited the most important first word in the man's occupation title because it didn't fit the first line, and she didn't consider the second line. But the box did have another line for answers appropriate to that question. Clearly line number fifteen, part of the Occupation box, showed an available line right below car builder that could have easily accommodated a three-word title like railroad car builder. But she'd hurried with her answer to line fourteen without considering line fifteen, and had already dismissed the R word, essentially hiding her error. There is no cure for indelible. The woman walks a fine line of error and dishonesty with obvious lack of respect for the work she is entrusted to perform. That she eliminated a word for convenience instead of taking time to handwrite to size created an untruth with permanence. It also allows possibility of unfortunate employment consequences. There were a few other errors too, already mentioned. But this is more than just misspelling a word: it is a deliberate decision to abolish a word—and even one word has power to alter a life—from a person's occupation title to permissions granted.

Thus, officially on the certificate of birth two words answer the father's occupation: car builder. And that suggests automobile mechanic without the qualifying first word, 'Railroad.' John's father built railroad cars. There is a big difference: steam turbines, electric locomotives, and diesel electric railroad cars required heft and skilled builders, unlike assembly lines for mass production of an entire automobile.

Regrettably, the difference, the error, cannot be corrected. The ink is indelible. So now, with two answers incomplete on the certificate of birth—occupation and missing middle name—we have two errors to add to the already three.

#

John, thankful for final success, doesn't see any worrisome blemishes on the document, only the beauty of a legal official certificate of birth. It is a replacement, not quite a duplicate, but offered as certain in its accuracy and entirety. The original had been badly soaked in a box with other faded flood papers capable in most cases of still revealing information from carefully pulled apart once wet pages. Never mind a substitute, this 1939 document feels magical in its owner's hand as he pets the unseen seal of his birth. They leave the office, envelope tight in Mabel's hand, and walk over to the car. They can go home now. But long hours of driving with a well past midnight arrival wouldn't be wise.

Mabel wants to see more of the document. Something caught her eye that still disturbs her. She's not sure, and Johnny didn't pick up on it, so she thinks alone that there may be a discrepancy in dates. A mile or so down the road, her curiosity building, she asks permission to reopen the document.

"Of course. But I don't want to engage right now," John says. "I need to keep driving. I'll take another look later, at dinner. By the way, I'd like to make tonight celebratory: a fine restaurant with all the trimmings."

Mabel's opening the envelope as he speaks, and immediately sees what she first noticed. "Johnny look at this," she blurts out, holding it up.

"Not now, please, Mabel. I don't want a collision, and I don't know the roads here at all. I'm also trying to look around for our evening accommodations: they have to be worthy of the last night of our treasured trip. Okay? I'm sorry to be so distracted."

"That's all right," she says, turning to him with a smile. "I understand, and tonight sounds great." She inserts the document back in the envelope, deciding it really isn't her place to read something so personal without its owner. She places it on his lap.

John drives in silence now, appreciating the rolling hills he sees beyond the city, taking in deep breaths of the serenity they give forth. And he looks over at Mabel, completion of an odyssey. With certificate at hand and fullness of heart, his raison d'etre is beautifully established. It has been a glorious day—absolute in validation of birth and family, celebrated by the early buds of spring. As if on cue, an old manor house with a vacancy sign beckons from the side road Johnny has just decided to explore. It looks perfect.

They're led to a white linen-covered table placed privately in the far corner of the restaurant overlooking the pond. Yes, perfect. Quaint and cozy, and with a full moon to shine in on Mabel. John decides to buy a camera very soon.

"So what is it, my dear, that troubles you?" Johnny asks, finally ready to relax. He has brought the envelope to the table and withdraws the certificate.

Mabel points to the error of dates she'd noticed earlier. "The year of birth, look at it, Johnny: 1913! You are a year younger than you thought, well, almost, with a birthday in June not July," she says.

"Oh, dear, this makes me 'the older woman!' What do I do?" And they laugh together, sort of. John is trying to process this unexpected revelation.

"Don't look so sad, Johnny," Mabel says. "Think how lucky you are to find an extra year of youth. Nobody gets a chance to go back in time." She stops. His face is expressionless: she's been glib, insensitive, and realizes it at once. That he'd known so little about himself, even his age and month of birth, is a bit of a shock.

"Isn't this what I came to find?" he reminds himself. "Knowledge about my heritage, my early years in Pennsylvania? Well, here it is: significant maybe, but doubtful. No need to agonize or analyze over it. I have Mabel now: we have our future and our faith. That's what really matters." He turns to her, so dear but nervously confused now, and pulls her close. The hug tells her he's okay, that everything will be fine.

"May I take your order?" the waiter asks.

After a delicious dinner and decadent dessert, followed by a lingering night of sweet nearness, Johnny and Mabel are headed home. He's pensive and it seems at least an hour before he finally speaks. "I don't know, Mabel, why I thought July: maybe because it's always hottest in July, Mama once said, and my party was outdoors on a very hot day; guess I equated it with the heat of July when I was asked about my birth by the Children's Aid person signing me in. But it's the difference in year that's most troubling. I wonder about it: how did it happen? Could it have been a clerical error? *Yes, it could have, especially knowing now of the error-prone woman that singularly prepared the certificate; but it's unlikely: her mistakes were more word-related than numerical.*

"You have no idea, Mabel, of how vivid that birthday memory is. All these years I've been able to recall the details: pretty wrapped presents, balloons all around, Mama's homemade decorated cake, ice cream too, and the challenge to blow out six little candles lighting my life that day.

I know there were six: I blew them out myself, though most likely with more than one breath. There is no doubt they were all there."

"Of course they were, darling. Your memory isn't at fault," Mabel says, softening her voice to the tune of sorrow. "What you saw that day, and all those nights you lay alone thinking back to your happy memory, are correct. You simply failed to take into account, because you never knew, is the birthday tradition of an extra candle on the cake for good luck. You turned five that year, Johnny: not six." And she bursts into tears. The ordeal is finally catching up to her: the unexpected telephone call, the rush into the city, the increasing web of deceit, a family divided; new people, new places, a renewed love so poignant…. She's tired and can't escape the weight of it all, the depth of compassion she feels for the man she loves so much. She thinks about her father, the other man she loves but now fears. She expects a war of words at the family home on Doughty Boulevard. But this time she cannot be coerced. She is different now: she knows with certainty the man with whom she wants to spend her life. Mabel is heart and soul in love with Johnny.

Chapter XXI

Mabel Eleanor Castle and John Frank Huszar were married on June 4, 1939. It was the Lord's Day, now their day too, and as bright and glorious as a sun ever shines. It was to be a simple ceremony with only family and close friends to first share the early service followed by wedding cake and tea in the fellowship hall. There were no invitations, only personal phone calls. Crowell was first on the list, for without her there would have been a formal announcement of Mabel's betrothal that night at the Christmas Ball, complete with happy guests' expectation to attend the glamorous dream wedding already floating in air, in error. This bride didn't need a fancy wedding gown: it was an understated to-the-knee white linen dress decorated only by the beauty of its fullness. Two attendants, Mabel's sisters, of course, were aglow with happiness. John had already endeared himself to the entire family. They saw character, startling intellect, humility, sensitivity, and ambition in this man, and less important, far less important, but maybe also noticed, the handsome good looks and easy manner.

With a unanimous Castle family apology, evidenced in their gratitude for Mabel's rebellion, albeit belatedly, against the misguided pressure on her to send him away, John was warmly welcomed into the fold. But the planned simplicity of a small private ceremony was lost to the crowds of well-wishers who had flocked outside the church when word of the Castle-Huszar wedding spread. Alfred personally walked back to the vestibule and opened the doors wide with invitation, stepping outside and waving them in. He greeted many familiar faces and many unknown but obviously not to his family. It was a remarkable expression of friendship and goodwill. As the visitors were getting seated, they respectfully muffled the sounds of motion. And very soon all was quiet.

Mabel still chose not to walk down the aisle with her father, instead entered from one side of the altar as John entered simultaneously from the opposite, recreating their walk to each other that beautiful night of Christmas joy and discovered love. Today they meet at the end of the aisle and step to the altar to speak the precious words of their hearts, joining hands for visible affirmation of their becoming one. And when the minister, the Rev. Dr. Roby Day, asked, "Who will give the bride away?" Alfred Castle took license with his answer: "I do with pride and gladness in my heart."

And Mabel's blue eyes always sparkling with diamond-cut brilliance glistened just a little bit more. The guests, doubled in size, followed the wedding party, by request, to the fellowship hall where a second towered wedding cake miraculously stood on the table: a gift that was never identified but perfectly on time to serve guests in the very fellowship hall where Mabel learned to love the story of five barley loaves and two fish.

The bride and groom took no honeymoon. They sought their own time in their new home, a time to remember the moments of excitement after a stranger giving a speech said the magic word that brought them together again, mindful of how close they came to losing their unclaimed love. The cottage was white with yellow shutters, set back beyond the main house on Avenue A in Inwood, with colorful flower gardens brightening the green expanse of lawn that was their front yard. The beautiful big white two-story farmhouse, hugged by a wide porch on three sides, was owned by Lewis Jackson's parents. They were known as Mom and Pop Jackson, beloved residents of Inwood, so it had a nice family feel that would someday blossom into to a favorite place for little cousins to play. Someone must have had artistic talent in order to cut wood into a rather intricate duck design. There were full grown and smaller size patterns arranged in typical 'mama leading ducklings' formation, painted yellow, naturally, but a nice match to the white cottage shutters, and well detailed with orange paint on their bills and black for their eyes. It was a child's maze. To complete the storybook scene was the ever-present white picket fence, beyond which wild sunflowers grew. They especially swayed close to the cottage, as if moving to music, serenading the newlyweds inside.

Most people described Mabel and John's first home a dollhouse. It was that adorable. And so much better than any hotel or ocean cruise for their honeymoon: it was home, where Mabel wanted to be, belonging to Johnny, joined to Johnny as his wife, in his bed, in their perfect love. For John it is the fruition of a double dream: (a) that one day he would come to know the girl in the kitchen, and (b) though unrealistic, that she could return his 'at first sight' love with her own. He did, she did, and with no uncertainty they are today ardent believers in the miracles of true love.

"Good night, Mrs. Huszar," John says, in hard-won triumph.

"Good night, darling husband," she sleepily answers.

Chapter XXII

"Hath this child been already baptized?" asked the Rev. Dr. Roby F. Day, and they answered, "No."

Little Janice has been very quiet in her seat. She may have been the only one of the private congregation in the nave that early afternoon without tears. Ella Castle, the grandmother, shed hers, allowing them to flow unabashedly. Alfred Castle was seen to dab at his eyes once or twice as well. Other family members and dear old friends and a host of new ones important in the lives of John and Mabel were there, some standing, others in a pew, all in support, and many straining against emotion. In the second row were the 'almost brothers' from The Farm, having traveled far for the joy of witnessing John's new family, complete with first child, submitting forever to God.

Dr. Day, minister at the font that held the Holy Water, began: "Dearly beloved, forasmuch as our Savior Christ saith, 'None can enter into the kingdom of God, except he be regenerate and born anew of Water and of the Holy Ghost; I beseech you to call upon God the Father, through our Lord Jesus Christ, that of his bounteous mercy he will grant to Janice Elizabeth Huszar that which by nature she cannot have; that she may be baptized with Water and the Holy Ghost, and received into Christ's holy Church, and be made a living member of the same." Concurrent to those words he dabbed Holy Water onto the little girl's forehead, not really expecting her sweet smile in return. "Let us pray."

And when the prayer was over and the words of the Gospel read, and the service for Janice concluded but not dismissed, the minister moved on to a second baptismal. That which is called Conditional Baptism for those where there is reasonable doubt whether he or she was baptized with water.

John kneels and bows his head for just a moment. And while it may have been without precedent, and not a proper part of the service, Janice, herself just baptized, was softly motioned to move to her daddy's right side and kneel down beside him while Mommy knelt at his left.

"If thou art not already baptized, John Frank Huszar, I baptize thee in the Name of the Father, and of the Son, and of the Holy Ghost. Amen."

And John, joined by his wife and daughter—his own real family—became members of the far larger family of God.

All in attendance were aware of the intensity of the moment. In fact, they were deeply moved. The Sacrament symbolized so much for John that day. And the guests felt it. Each knows his story and how very special the man—not just his story—truly is. Save for the sounds of muffled sobs and choked-back coughs escaping even the best of men, there was silence in St. Paul's Methodist Church of Inwood, a reverence unbroken for several moments of personal prayer. Indeed it was a time to be still: and a time to be thankful.

The gently sloping landscaped grounds at the Castle home provided a perfect setting for an outdoor luncheon and refreshments following the somber service. Card tables set up under a portable canopy offered guests an array of fine foods. And especially, but not for long, on the table of temptation is John's favorite dessert: the unequalled 'Aunt Edith's yellow layer cake' with vanilla pudding between and milk chocolate icing on top. It was a guilty pleasure desired by many. The host and hostess, Mom and Dad to John for more than three years now and very comfortable in their roles, were happily serving their guests. It made Mabel smile.

She and John savored the convivial atmosphere, alive with music and happy chatter in a seamless transfer from formality to festivity. John strode among the tables greeting each and every visitor, thanking them for being a part of the very special day. And then he walked back to the big house with his little daughter in hand and put her down for a nap. From that distance, not very far of course, just enough for a panoramic view, he stood for a few minutes deep in thought. So many blessings, so many feelings . . . Johnny from the streets all grown up. So he stayed a while, just watching. His eyes always go back to Mabel, finding her easily in any crowd or forest trail. She was already more beautiful today than ever before, even at their wedding. For now she is maturing into true womanly grace. Still slender, today she is wearing a polka dot silk shirtdress: beige and navy, with a straw hat and tan toe spectator heels to complement the look. Little Janice wore a white bodice dress with pink sash until arriving back at Nana's house where her mother fast changed her into the simplicity of washable play clothes.

"It was nice of you, Mr. Eckard, to drive all the way down for this occasion," John says. "Our cottage is tiny, but I know that the Jacksons, Mom and Pop to us all, have plenty of room for you to stay overnight. We live on their property, steps behind them, and are connected by marriage so we feel like family. Have you met them? May I introduce you if not?"

"How kind of you, Johnny, to think of my comfort, but I have made plans with an old colleague from our Schermerhorn days. We will meet for dinner together, and then I will go to a long-ago favorite inn where I already have a reservation. But thank you. My friend is quite lonely having lost his wife within the last year, and I am experienced in similar grief. I think my words, or just presence, might encourage him."

"Yes sir, I'm certain you will be of great help. I have known for quite some time that you are alone, and offer again my condolences for your loss. I hope that Stephen and Peg live near enough to be part of your life," John adds.

"Well, they are not nearby. Peg lives in Binghamton with her husband and three sons that are all involved in sports and studies. Holidays are enjoyed together every other year in fairness to the grandparents who live in California. Stephen studied in England and decided to live there. I say it's a good thing I love to read.

"Margaret was my partner so her loss remains significant in my life. She has been dead many years now. She took ill soon after you moved down here. The doctors on board said her mind had snapped and that she would require full time nursing home care. So I put her in a nearby facility, up in Albany, and visited—though unknown to her—as much as possible until rapid physical deterioration took her further, and finally, from me.

"But enough of an unpleasant theme: I came to honor you and meet your beautiful wife and daughter. They have lifted my heart."

As Baynard is talking, Johnny is thinking … "Darn, the man looks so thin and lost without her. That he came alone says a lot: it gives credence to my position in that family. No, not 'that' family: 'my' family; and not a 'position' but a 'part of.' His attendance here today says I was more than a favored boarding student. I was important to both of them, and that feels good." So with reassurance he ends this moment of reflection, thankful for its messenger. And free of blame. John accompanies Baynard to his car with a promise to relay the man's pleasure of meeting Mabel and daughter and his gratitude for the thoughtful invitation to the event. He's leaving early due to the need to nap at the inn prior to meeting his friend for dinner. To walk back to where the busy work of serving foods, sweets, and beverages to the many guests still going strong would be to interfere and also an effort for Baynard, now using a cane. And he has already enjoyed the delicacies of lunch and a dessert of fresh berries. The car is parked out front on Doughty Boulevard: the men shake hands first, then pat each other's shoulders in deeper meaning, and Baynard then moves into his seat. John locks the car door and watches part of his past drive away, realizing that most likely it has been their last time together.

John returns to his guests, first focusing on Crowell deep in conversation at the punch bowl. She's retired now but as full of life as ever. Widowed with no children or grandchildren for companionship or legacy, she must be lonely at times. She told John earlier that she was considering returning to Nova Scotia where she was born and educated. That suggests an empty life and a need to be with surviving family members. Most have died. But a younger sibling with several grown children and two cousins near her age would be there to provide warmth of memory and closeness of kin. After almost fifty years living in the same apartment on Second Avenue in New York City trekking daily to Far Rockaway, she is too attached to leave, for this is really home. The decision she keeps delaying is very difficult, but eventually Crowell does return to her roots. John makes a mental note: "Must invite Crowell over for Sunday dinner very soon."

And Duke, bless his devilish heart, has long since recovered from the humiliation of rejection by Mabel, dining often now at her Sunday afternoon ritual: turkey and ham, and fresh greens every week are basic, while accessory foods follow the season. Modeling Aunt Arlene Montgomery, Mabel sets the food on the dining table, keeping a low warm on the stove if required, and delights in the flow of family and friends that stop by. She had played matchmaker for her best friend, Alva, and the blind date with Duke blossomed into marriage. They happily announced last week that they're expecting their first child. It's especially joyous after their two years of trying.

The couples finally grew close after a time of distance between John and Duke that began long ago before John met Mabel. The fracture of friendship was the result of Duke's sabotage with an unforgiving lie that had hurt John enough to stay away. But for the sake of Mabel's relationships and the forgiveness his faith expects, he did the right thing. And they have enjoyed the mended fence these recent years; in fact, John offered Duke a job, and he has been a faithful loyal employee ever since. John's musings are still in play. But his back insists on a change of position, so he walks around the house to unstiffen a bit, absentmindedly sitting down on the front porch steps. New feelings surface, or are they the old?

He sits alone. How odd, not one person has interrupted the reverie. He glances around and begins to feel a little uncomfortable with the carefree and untouched lives resplendent on the lawn in front of him.

So much abundance here when in other parts of the world there is severe hunger and disease, insufficient shelter, and warring nations with enormous loss of life. He is troubled by ongoing devastation of war still raging in the Pacific theater. Hundreds of thousands of young men just like himself—except not yet fathers, and without heart murmurs—are dying in the Pacific and facing disastrous consequences in Europe and North Africa…. Two friends from Spring Valley were killed he just learned from one of the upstate friends here today; plus two from Inwood and one from Far Rockaway have recently been added to the neighborhood list of heroes. He should be out there somewhere too, he feels, but he tried to volunteer, went to the recruitment desk to enlist, only to be designated 4-F because of the heart murmur. And at that juncture, even without the medical issue, he would have been denied due to automatic placement on the deferment list for those with dependent children. But he would willingly fight for his country, sacrifice what is so dear now, his family, if only he were allowed to serve. Maybe later, if need be and restrictions are relaxed: he may be called back they said. One day they might have to replenish from a second tier list, and he could be on it. For now, though, the little exemption is upstairs peacefully asleep on her grandparents' bed, keeping her daddy safe at home. He went upstairs to check on his daughter. She is perfectly beautiful. And he etched the moment in his memory. Another mental portrait: another image for forever. She is his lifeblood, this child at the center of his attention: the only one here actually sharing with him the same blood and history. She is Austria; she is Renovo. She is both Frank and Lizzie. She is all he has of his heritage. The ache in his soul is the possibility, though admittedly unlikely, that three others, or at least one of three, could have been within age to be a precious elder in this gathering. Other than his deceased parents, the missing family members are Lizzie's two sisters and a brother who were denied the little boy they loved. John wonders if they married, and were there children, and how did the family grow? *Watch out, Johnny. Remember when you realized as a young boy that there are always blessings to count? They might not be first choice, what you covet, but they deserve to be counted.* Ashamed for a moment, John soon agrees with his conscience. He has so many blessings, so many answered prayers, there's no need for more. And that's not who he really is: he has always been a grateful person.

It's just that the desire to know one's roots is innate. Later, when not so busy building a career and providing for his family, John will dedicate more time to following the footsteps of his family. Somebody may still be out there, old friend from school, parishioner from the Catholic Church, a shopkeeper with customer records in hard cover ledgers out back.... Among the many friendly residents of the little city there should be someone who recognizes the Huszar or Illar name, maybe even has a link to someone who was acquainted with the families. John has called Pennsylvania and Ohio newspaper headquarters and routinely purchases old issues by mail; and every business trip is ripe for reading local telephone books. The quest is current. At one point, John traced the sisters to Philadelphia where records indicated both had resided for a couple of years. Then he learned they had migrated to Ohio and decided it was a good time to suspend his search a while. That was wise. He has to be careful that a mission does not become a burden. Allow for the beauty of each season, the comfort of friends, the love of family, and if we look more closely, the little everyday miracles.

"I have no right to spend time in my past," Johnny repeats regularly in the mirror.

Nap time over, they are walking to him now. And at the sight of mother and child, John's heart fills with love and gratitude as he calls out to them, "Come on, you two. Hurry!"

"We've missed you," Mabel says, giving her beloved a quick kiss and lifting Janice up into his arms. "Everything okay, honey?" she asks.

"Yes, my love I'm fine. Everything's fine," John says because it is. Everything is good. Holding his daughter close, face to face, he touches nose to nose and she giggles; he loves the sound of her delight. His eyes move up to meet her eyes, sun-speckled brown and already as haunting and expressive as his: perfect duplicates of grandmother Lizzie's eyes according to Papa when he said that of John's own. It is pure ancestry Johnny sees shining through. He looks next at his wife, her face always radiant against the red highlights in her hair: the first of her beauty one sees. They, the little family, hurry to join their guests, all greeted earlier and enjoying the best of life. It's a lovely afternoon.

It's a Sunday.

The End

CPSIA information can be obtained
at www.ICGtesting.com
Printed in the USA
LVHW080430290520
656858LV00004B/14

9 781400 327096